ADAPT OR DIE

YOUR SURVIVAL GUIDE TO
MODERN WAREHOUSE AUTOMATION

ADAPT

OR DIE

JEREMY BODENHAMER

HOUNDSTOOTH
PRESS

ADAPT OR DIE

Your Survival Guide to Modern Warehouse Automation

ISBN   978-1-5445-1712-4 *Hardcover*
        978-1-5445-1711-7 *Paperback*
        978-1-5445-1710-0 *Ebook*

To the leaders of every business trying to compete against the giants. You are the ones building our communities and feeding our families. It's you who give us our strength.

CONTENTS

INTRODUCTION

Are you an e-commerce executive? A retailer, manufacturer, or distributor? Are you wondering how you can afford to meet faster and faster delivery times and ever-escalating customer expectations? Are you nervous that your business may not exist in five years as Amazon and its global competitors continue their efforts to copy your products, steal your customers, circumvent your secret sauce, and wipe you off the map?

This book is for you!

Operations have been overlooked for too long. There are countless books on sales and marketing, but very few on logistics. What the sales and marketing books fail to mention is that very few sales and marketing efforts can be successful without a strong operations component behind the buy button.

Untold billions are pouring into post-sale operations. Today's warehouses are no longer the tired, dark spaces they once were. They teem with life, both real and artificial. That old, dusty workplace is now the epicenter of a global revolution.

I'm sure you are imagining hundreds of colorful warehouse robots wheeling through narrow aisles and between towering floor-to-ceiling pallet stacks. But this isn't you. You don't have robots, and you still think AI is a Spielberg movie, not a strategic business weapon. You know facilities like these are real, but in your world, warehouse automation and its components are less *iRobot* and more *The Office*.

So the big questions are: how is your business going to compete in a world where the competition is able to invest hundreds of millions in each next-gen warehouse? Where they have their own private force of delivery drivers? Where they control all the data?

If you are a larger shipper, how are you going to transition from a world of legacy software, static rules, and single-sourced carrier loyalty to the dynamic operation that will be required for your survival? Your business is at risk too!

These are the questions we hope to answer in this book.

WAREHOUSE AUTOMATION IS THE SOLUTION FOR THESE CHALLENGES

Yes, the world has changed, and it feels like the speed of change is accelerating. However, there are solutions, even for fighting the largest giants.

A friend of mine manufactures and sells to all the big players—brick-and-mortar, e-commerce, direct to consumer (DTC), and on marketplaces. He faced similar competitive threats on Amazon like those mentioned above. But it's not just Amazon who knocks-off products. "Walmart, Target, Best Buy, they all do it," he told me. "If your sales are crushing it, they will knock you off with their own private label product. We have about a year before we need to bring them a better product to get the top spot again."

"The one thing I learned is that you constantly have to innovate and reinvent yourself."

That is precisely what we are here to do. This doesn't just apply to R&D, but to warehousing, shipping, and fulfillment as well.

There are companies today who are absolutely killing it in spite of Amazon's crazy war chest and questionable business practices. One example we will discuss involves a company going head-to-head with Amazon, selling core CPG (consumer packaged goods) products, and winning. When I met them not many years ago, they were just a few people in a small, cramped office. Today, in spite of Amazon's continued dominance, their company is valued at more than $1 billion.

AUTOMATION TODAY AND TOMORROW

"She's been a dance-floor cowgirl. A disco diva in leg warmers. A punky bubblegum pop star. An erotic mistress. A spiritual guru. An American dream girl. A rebel heart." This from an MTV news article on the master of reinvention, Madonna, who "has both defined and redefined what it means to be a pop star, a performer, and an icon."[1]

You may hate my example, but just as Madonna has adapted over time to remain on top of the music world, we must continue to adapt to stay competitive in our world of e-commerce and distri-

---

1   Erica Russell, "Why Madonna's Legacy of Reinvention Is More Relevant than Ever," *MTV News*, last modified April 24, 2019, http://www.mtv.com/news/3121740/madonna-legacy-madame-x-reinvention/.

bution. It may seem like an odd comparison, but history tells us that if we don't adapt, we will die, soon to be replaced by a younger, prettier, more popular star who can get products to customers faster and cheaper.

To this end, we will break our evolution discussion into three parts.

In Part 1, we will discuss the e-commerce and warehouse environments as they are today. It is critical to understand the competitive landscape prior to diving into the strategic details.

Part 2 goes inside the operation and main components of warehouse automation: shipping, packing, warehousing, data and analytics, robotics, and operations workers. Supply chain publications usually speak about shipping software in three buckets: planning, execution, and visibility. Although all areas are discussed in various capacities, they are done so from the perspective of a shipper's pains and challenges and steps they should take in order to mitigate specific competitive threats.

Part 3 talks about the future and how to best prepare your business model for long-term sustainable growth.

I know it's hard to believe, but Madonna is in her sixties and still selling pop albums. The truth is, "...she remains relevant because, quite frankly, she's still here; still uncompromising and still reinventing; still flipping off a culture that seeks to push her out."[2] This is exactly what we want to accomplish for your business by giving you the tools to ensure you are around for many years to come.

---

[2]   Ibid.

WAREHOUSE AUTOMATION AND ME

My family never owned a multigenerational shipping company, and I wasn't an early Amazon employee. In fact, one of my closest advisors, a Wharton grad and successful startup founder, once referred to me as a nobody from nowhere. I don't have an Ivy League degree, and before my adventure into logistics, I knew nothing about shipping, fulfillment, packaging, inventory, ERPs, or product distribution. Yet for some reason, I thought it would be a good idea to buy a failing, off-brand pack-and-ship store in sunny Santa Barbara, California a few months after my twenty-sixth birthday.

On my first day working in the store, a man walked in with a life-sized wooden rocking horse. It was at least six feet tall and capable of rocking two grown men. It was the depth of the Great Recession; he had lost his house and was selling off everything on eBay. He asked if I could ship the horse to the buyer. Knowing nothing about freight or freight brokers, I said yes. That fateful decision determined my path for the next fourteen years.

It took me a little over two years to grow the pack-and-ship business into a top performer. By 2011, my phone was ringing off the hook with customers asking me one question: "How much does the shipping cost?"

So, I did what any small business shipping professional would do. I sold my business, raised venture capital, and started building shipping software to answer the question. Our mission is to create a world where shipping positively impacts society without thrashing workers, our environment, or the bottom line. Today, ShipHawk, a parcel and LTL transportation management system (TMS), processes millions of shipments. Each year, my sales team and I speak with thousands of companies and analyze millions of transactions in an effort to drill down on the strategies businesses are using to win in today's market. Some of these stories are shared herein.

AUTOMATION'S FAR-EXTENDING REACH

I wrote this book for e-commerce and operations owners, executives, and teams, because automation impacts all of us—from the small, independent business owner looking to better package her products, to the mid-market distribution center moving hundreds of thousands or even millions of shipments a month that are looking to make sense of byzantine shipping rules and regulations. Retailers, manufacturers, and distributors all face automation challenges.

Automation does not just affect business owners and executives. In many ways, automation's most direct impacts are felt by those working daily in DCs (distribution centers, also known as fulfillment centers, FCs, or more generically, warehouses), whose labor could become less precarious and more fulfilling—both economically and physically—by way of automation done right.

Automation's predicted impact on humanity is so great that a famous venture capitalist and a prominent tech journalist wrote a seminal book on it, which I cite several times. To be clear, these guys aren't like us. As founder of Mohr Davidow Ventures, William Davidow is one of the guys investing in automation at all levels and across many sectors. He's someone with an inside look at the pipeline of forthcoming technologies that many of us can't yet see. Michael Malone has been writing about technology since the 1980s and teaches about its impact at the university level. In their book, *The Autonomous Revolution: Reclaiming the Future We've Sold to Machines*, they detail the rise of artificial intelligence and predict automation's impact on humans as capable of "spark[ing] a wholesale breakdown of civil society."

However, we can't just talk about warehouse automation without acknowledging the rest of the world around us. The game of retail itself is changing, and success in the future will require a radical evolution of the independent business model. The world has never seen change at this pace, dealt with competitors with such a massive advantage, nor experienced the potentially devastating effects of automation on humanity. "A change so sweeping and complete as to be unlike anything we have ever experienced before," Davidow and Malone write. "It is almost beyond imagination."

One might argue that this is simply progress, that mature institutions are always becoming obsolete and being replaced. But you would have to look deeply into human history to find another era when almost *every* institution faces an existential challenge.

By every institution, I mean everyone, including you and your business. There is a group of powerful companies whose reach, now extending far beyond e-commerce and traditional brick-and-mortar retail, now threatens *all of us.*

The outsized investments of those few major players are driven by equally outsized business numbers. Three of these companies, who are also three of the top online marketplaces in the world—Amazon, Walmart, and Alibaba's collection of marketplaces including B2C and B2B platforms—are so big and generate such mind-boggling traffic and sales that it really only makes sense to speak of them relative to one another. By the end of 2019, Amazon was on track to deliver 3.5 billion packages by the year's end.[3] These 3.5 billion packages were produced at least in part by Amazon's 150 million mobile users,

---

3   Hayley Peterson, "Amazon's Delivery Business Reveals Staggering Growth as It's on Track to Deliver 3.5 Billion Packages Globally This Year," *Business Insider*, last modified December 19, 2019, https://www.businessinsider.com/amazon-package-delivery-business-growth-2019-12.

supposedly 119,928,851 products,[4] and, as of February 2020, upwards of two billion site visits per month. Unlike the other two companies, Walmart began as and continues to be a significant brick-and-mortar business. Not only do 90 percent of Americans live within fifteen miles of a Walmart, with an average of 275 million global visits per month in 2019,[5] and, also as of 2019, Walmart's omnichannel offerings generated an average of $4 million per hour, or $100 million per day for the Walton family behind Walmart.[6] Alibaba, whose presence in the West is growing, accounted for just over 55 percent of China's total e-commerce market as of May 2019.[7] On Singles' Day of 2019 (a shopping holiday on November 11), Alibaba infamously "logged more than 268 billion yuan ($38.3 billion)," though it vowed to ship its sales more conscientiously after receiving criticism for previously shipping one billion packages in one day.[8]

On their own, small and midsize businesses cannot compete with numbers like these, and they are often left with no other option than joining these very platforms as third-party vendors.

4   Maryam Mohsin, "10 Amazon Statistics You Need to Know in 2020," *Oberlo*, last modified April 7, 2020, https://www.oberlo.com/blog/amazon-statistics.

5   "Number of Weekly Customer Visits to Walmart Stores Worldwide from Fiscal Year 2017 to 2020 (in Millions of Customer Visits)," Statista, last modified April 2, 2020, https://www.statista.com/statistics/818929/number-of-weekly-customer-visits-to-walmart-stores-worldwide/.

6   Nicole Lyn Pesce, "The Walton Family Gets $100 Million Richer Every Single Day," MarketWatch, last modified August 17, 2019, https://www.marketwatch.com/story/the-walton-family-gets-100-million-richer-every-single-day-2019-08-12.

7   "Leading B2C Retailers' Share of Sales in Total Retail e-Commerce Sales in China as of May 2019," Statista, last modified February 13, 2020, https://www.statista.com/statistics/880212/sales-share-of-the-leading-e-commerce-retailers-in-china/.

8   Lulu Yilun Chen, "Alibaba Seals $38 Billion Singles' Day Sales Record," Bloomberg, last modified November 10, 2019, https://www.bloomberg.com/news/articles/2019-11-10/alibaba-hits-6-billion-yuan-of-singles-day-sales-in-a-minute.

This market concentration is one of the reasons entrepreneurship is declining in high-income countries. "Incumbent firms have a growing amount of power that stops new ones from entering the market."[9]

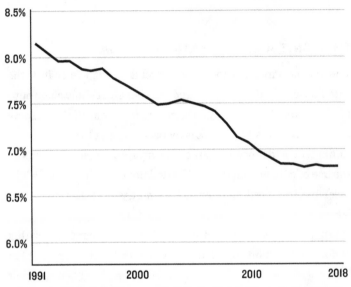

Wim Naudé, "The Decline of Entrepreneurship in the West: Is Complexity Ossifying the Economy?" *IZA Institute of Labor Economics*, DP no. 12602 (September 2019): 3, http://ftp.iza.org/dp12602.pdf.

Even as our world changes, and even as the pace of that change accelerates, the reality is that small and midsize companies build communities and feed families. Independent businesses are essential. To keep pace with the change, they must adapt, automate, and take control of the technology at their disposal because as Davidow and Malone point out, "One thing is certain, if we choose to treat phase change as business as usual, we will all become its victims."

---

9   Wim Naudé, "The Surprising Decline of Entrepreneurship and Innovation in the West," *The* Conversation, last modified October 8, 2019, https://theconversation.com/the-surprising-decline-of-entrepreneurship-and-innovation-in-the-west-124552.

The goal of this book is to present the landscape as it is today, with a few major players using hard to replicate tactics and massive war chests in order to thin the competitive herd and to present the steps businesses must consider if they are to survive the competitive onslaught.

THIS ISN'T AN AUTOMATION MANUAL

The transportation and logistics market is too big, even within the warehouse, for this book to be a comprehensive supply chain automation manual. The supply chain is automating at all stages, some faster than others. This book is focused on parcel and LTL, order fulfillment, and tangential areas like inventory management and the use of data and analytics. We will not cover inbound freight, receiving, truckload, or other still relevant, yet out-of-scope topics.

One more note before we get started. Let me be clear up front; this is not a book about Amazon (even though I will mention them almost 400 times). As of this writing, Amazon owns 35–40 percent of the US e-commerce market, and COVID is fueling faster-than-ever growth while obliterating the remaining brick-and-mortar businesses who have managed to stay alive this long.[10] Their immense size and power require us to use them as a barometer for future decision-making, strategy blueprints, and good old-fashioned gamesmanship.

With proper planning, leveraging of available technologies, and a desire to adapt, your business can survive and thrive. Delivery times, order throughput, customer loyalty, and the welfare of your

---

10 Karen Weise, "Amazon Angles to Grab Back Customers," *The New York Times*, last modified May 22, 2020, https://www.nytimes.com/2020/05/22/technology/amazon-coronavirus-target-walmart.html.

workers can all be improved. By focusing on these areas, you can make your business more money, not less.

That being said, winning in this market will require a major perspective change, and the new perspective is the first step in ensuring that the operations teams that are critical to the success of your business and the health and vitality of the communities in which you operate will no longer be overlooked. The world behind the buy button has never been more important. My hope is that after reading this book, the warehouse(s) in your operation will serve as the driving force for positive, sustainable, profitable, and ethical change, making you a leader in your industry.

PART I

THE CRISIS IN RETAIL...AND MANUFACTURING... AND DISTRIBUTION... AND...

CHAPTER 1

THE CURRENT TRUTH

HOW ARE YOU GOING TO COMPETE?

I'm the father of three boys, and our favorite man-time each week is on Saturday morning when we share a giant box of fancy donuts and watch *The Flash*. Even though I'm a huge fan of sugar-covered donuts, I'm not one to sugarcoat the truth, so I'm going to hit you straight: You AREN'T Amazon.

Your idea is great. Your product rocks. Your customers love you. Your team is smart and driven. You've invested tens of thousands, hundreds of thousands, even millions of dollars into your business.

Unfortunately, it doesn't matter. The five massive e-commerce giants have their sights set right on you.

You are an independent merchant. You are a manufacturer who spent many years and many more dollars to perfect your processes. You are a distributor who treats your employees with respect, pays them well, and builds strong customer relationships. You, the business founder or operator who overcame great odds, created jobs, built wealth, and spent your career making the world a better place are now in the center of their crosshairs.

To make matters worse, they have already pulled the trigger. The bullets are in flight. Some have hit their targets and killed. A rare few have missed, and the rest will be hitting daily until everyone has been converted or destroyed. It doesn't matter who you are. Your time is limited. The writing is on the wall. Even if you don't feel it yet, they are coming for you.

We can't afford to ignore their power, their influence, and their near-universal domination. Small and medium-sized businesses are the bedrock of our society. They feed families. They build communities. How can we ensure they survive? How do we ensure they thrive? How are they going to compete?

THE LIKELY FUTURE—THE FIVE APIS OF THE APOCALYPSE

I predict a possible and *very real* future scenario without independent merchants. One with five e-commerce engines (who we will affectionately refer to as the Big 5)—Amazon, Alibaba, Walmart, JD.com and Shopify—that will run global commerce. Every product. Every transaction. Every dollar spent.

I predict a possible and *very real* future scenario for consumers with few buying options, little meaningful competition, and commerce giants so big and powerful that every interaction feels like sitting on hold with the cable company waiting for help with your internet outage. Sure, it doesn't feel like this today, because they need us. Yet in the future, they won't. We will need them. We won't be able to buy products locally (already true). Most sellers will push entire product catalogs to marketplace majors (already happening). Oh, and costs will rise, and rise, and rise (also already happening). Maybe you heard of the COVID-related hand sanitizer price gouging? For the record, they blamed it on the AI.

The Big 5 is about dominance, power, and ubiquity. More important, though, each member of the Big 5 has a unique vision of what the future should look like.

If you happen to like the versions of the future they represent— for example, instant gratification at tremendous expense with Jeff Bezos or increased surveillance with Jack Ma—then these outcomes are beneficial or at least not negative. If you don't, it may be too late.

Some members of the Big 5 may claim to make decisions with humanity's best interests at heart, while their data may suggest otherwise, or that they don't at all. When I say best interests, I don't mean low prices, as you will see. At this stage of human evolution, low prices alone are a sure path to destruction.

A few of these powerhouse players don't want to corner the market. They want to *become* the market. They already own the factories, planes, ships, trucks, warehouses, sorting facilities, distribution centers, the vans that speed through your neighborhood, the digital infrastructure the entire system lives on, and all the data on every customer who has ever clicked, researched, bought, sold, returned, or otherwise engaged with them.

Their Smart speakers, video-doorbells, and integrated cameras are already recording every word uttered within the confines of every sacred space. A spoken product name, even by a child, can result in an unexpected, near immediate, delivery.

I WANT A DOLLHOUSE!

On her family's Amazon Echo, a six-year-old girl from Dallas, Texas inadvertently "placed an order" with Alexa for four pounds of cookies and a dollhouse. In fact, as California news channel CW-6 covered the story, "It accidentally caused a slew of other Alexas to also attempt shopping sprees." As the TV anchor said, "I love the little girl saying, 'Alexa ordered me a dollhouse.'" Amazon Echoes in the viewers' homes started placing orders for dollhouses.[11]

The insane and invasive competitive advantage doesn't end with near-ubiquitous order placement. Amazon has spent up to US $200 million on each new eighth-generation fulfillment center to fulfill these frictionless orders.[12] In addition, they already operate more than 100 such warehouses in North America and 185 globally.[13] Warehouses that, since 2014, "feature cutting-edge technology and robotics."[14]

Very few shippers can afford to set up semi-intelligent ordering devices in customers' homes, operate more than 100 domestic warehouses, invest $200 million in each new DC, or supply cutting-edge robotics at scale, yet they must still meet the same

11 Ananya Bhattacharya, "Amazon's Alexa Heard Her Name and Tried to Order up a Ton of Dollhouses," Quartz, last modified January 7, 2017, https://qz.com/880541/amazons-amzn-alexa-accidentally-ordered-a-ton-of-dollhouses-across-san-diego/.

12 Casey Coombs, "Amazon to spend $200M for one of its most expensive fulfillment centers ever (Video)," June 9, 2017. *Puget Sound Business Journal.* Online, https://www.bizjournals.com/seattle/news/2017/06/09/amazon-to-spend-200m-on-fulfillment-center-for-130.html.

13 Nate Rattner and Annie Palmer, "This map shows how Amazon's warehouses are rapidly expanding across the country," *CNBC*, last modified January 19, 2020, https://www.cnbc.com/2020/01/19/map-of-amazon-warehouses.html.

14 "Amazon's fulfillment network," About Amazon, last accessed October 11, 2020, https://www.aboutamazon.com/working-at-amazon/amazons-fulfillment-network.

buyer expectations and get their orders to the customer's door in the same time frames.

To make matters worse, Amazon is now bypassing traditional shipping carriers like FedEx and UPS. A December 2019 article from *The Verge* stated, "Amazon is delivering half its own packages as it becomes a serious rival to FedEx and UPS. At the current rate, Amazon is set to pass both FedEx and UPS in US package volume, with the company currently delivering 2.5 billion packages per year compared to FedEx's three billion and UPS's 4.7 billion."[15] And they advertise free same-day deliveries in over 5,000 cities and towns.[16]

Christopher Cartelli, vice president of operations at Verishop and previous vice president of parcel operations and services at Newgistics believes "Businesses who can't offer same-day and next-day as their default delivery service will be gone within five years." I'm not sure how they will even last that long.

These services are relevant because the investment behind them is so large that no independent operator can compete. From June to September 2019, Amazon spent $9.6 billion on shipping and fulfillment.[17] It's like participating in a race from Los Angeles to New York, and the Big 5 are flying jets while the rest of us are riding bicycles.

---

15   Nick Statt, "Amazon Is Delivering Half Its Own Packages as It
     Becomes a Serious Rival to FedEx and UPS," *The* Verge, last modified
     December 13, 2019, https://www.theverge.com/2019/12/13/21020938/
     amazon-logistics-prime-air-fedex-ups-package-delivery-more-than-50-percent.

16   "Same-Day Delivery," Amazon, last accessed October 11, 2020, https://www.amazon.com/
     Prime-FREE-Same-Day-Delivery/b?ie=UTF8&node=8729023011.

17   Taylor Soper, "Amazon Will Spend Nearly $1.5B in Q4 for One-Day Delivery Initiative as Shipping
     Costs Skyrocket," GeekWire, last modified October 24, 2019, https://www.geekwire.com/2019/
     amazon-will-spend-nearly-1-5b-q4-one-day-delivery-initiative-shipping-costs-skyrocket/.

CHAPTER 2

THE DRIVING FORCE

BUYERS WANT IT EASY
AND WANT IT FAST

My oldest son ran into my home office the other day. "Daddy, daddy, did you know that they don't have Origami paper at Michaels?" Caught a little off guard, I stared at him trying to figure out the urgency. "They haven't had any in three years!" he exclaimed. "Do you know where else I can get some?"

"Online," I told him.

"That's what I was thinking," he replied, "but I don't want to get it online because it takes soooo long. Like three or four days."

So true, my little friend, so true. Three or four days does feel like a long time in a world of instant gratification and two-hour delivery promises. This is one of the reasons shipping has become the most crucial component of warehouse automation.

Amazon gets a lot of the credit for creating the systems and the infrastructure, but the real demand is coming from us, the buyers.

Whether it's a bike or a burrito, we want our stuff easy and we want it fast.

Before 2005, when Amazon first launched Prime, two-day shipping was considered something akin to rush delivery, and it was costly for both the shipper and the customer.[18] Not only were the most-needed items sitting on local retailer shelves, but when online orders were placed, customers were happy to get them delivered within a week. One- or two-day services were so expensive they were usually unthinkable. Now, fifteen years later, most customers expect either free, two-day, or free two-day shipping. In an attempt to exceed market expectations they themselves created, Amazon announced in early 2019 the introduction of one-day shipping for Prime customers, a change the company expects will cost roughly $800 million in the first quarter, and more later.[19] This is in addition to the same-day delivery offered through Amazon Prime Now in most major metropolitan areas.

What happened to the competition when Amazon made the one-day shipping announcement? Shares of Walmart and Target fell precipitously as the market reacted to the difficulty of delivering on this feat.[20] Walmart had no choice but to immediately get to work on their own expedited delivery service.[21]

---

18   Gaby Del Valle, "Amazon Created the Expectation of 2-Day Shipping. Now It Needs to Scale Back," Vox, last modified April 24, 2019, https://www.vox.com/the-goods/2019/4/23/18508093/amazon-prime-two-day-shipping.

19   Karen Weise, "Amazon's Profit Falls Sharply as Company Buys Growth," *The New York* Times, last modified October 24, 2019, https://www.nytimes.com/2019/10/24/technology/amazon-earnings.html.

20   Lauren Thomas, "Walmart, Target Shares Tumble as Amazon Announces One-Day Shipping for Prime Members," *CNBC*, last modified April 26, 2019, https://www.cnbc.com/2019/04/26/amazons-free-one-day-shipping-puts-the-pressure-on-walmart-target.html.

21   Jason Del Rey, "Walmart Is Quietly Working on an Amazon Prime Competitor Called Walmart+," *Vox*, last modified February 27, 2020, https://www.vox.com/recode/2020/2/27/21154357/walmart-plus-walmart-grocery-delivery-unlimited-membership-amazon-prime.

Amazon Prime members loved the announcement (remember, that's you and me!) because that means we get our stuff faster.

Research has shown that the "majority of buyers refuse to shop from a retailer following a negative delivery experience," which slow shipping times contribute to. The reality is that most buyers only judge shipping carriers by on-time deliveries. Shipping and delivery are near the top of consumer priorities, and "loyal customers [are] worth up to ten times as much as the value of their first purchase" and "increasing customer retention even by 5 percent could lead to increased profits of between 25 percent and 95 percent."[22] The Big 5 know that rapid delivery times help them gain and retain new customers—customers that used to be your customers.

SLOW SHIPPING KILLS

Crazy story for you to illustrate exactly how extreme our expectations have become. A friend of mine who runs customer success for a direct-to-consumer (D2C/DTC) brand found herself in the middle of serious delivery delays following the e-commerce boom during the COVID pandemic. She had no direct control over the order fulfillment processes or carrier routing, so she handled the situation by sending out discount codes for future purchases. Any customer who waited more than ten days to receive an order got a code for as much as 50 percent off their next purchase. How many were redeemed out of the 13,000 codes her team distributed? Only a hundred! What does this mean? This extremely low redemption rate suggests that customers completely abandoned the brand because of slow shipping! As I tell my boys, this is bananas!

---

22 Rohan Rinaldo Felix, "The Real Impact of Late Deliveries & How to Handle Them," *LateShipment.com*, last accessed October 11, 2020, https://www.lateshipment.com/blog/what-is-the-real-cost-of-delivering-packages-late/.

They also know nobody likes to pay for shipping. Buyers' experiences of shipping services rarely equate to the real cost of delivery, unless there is an urgent need. Think wedding dress on the wedding day. In that circumstance, the shipping value is almost priceless. Any cost sounds reasonable. However, your order of razor blades and pimple cream doesn't meet the same value threshold. In fact, we find almost no value in routine, day-to-day shipping services, which is precisely why sellers have rapidly adopted free shipping policies. Of the approximately 75 percent of customers whom e-commerce sites lose through cart abandonment, the number one reason given is unexpected shipping costs.[23] One could argue that in today's environment, any shipping cost is unexpected. According to a 2016 survey, free shipping, more than any other factor, would persuade customers to buy from e-commerce sites more frequently.[24]

Although almost no retailer can compete with the Big 5 on this or most other fronts, in 2018, Amazon spent US $27.7 billion—more than the GDP of 100 countries[25]—on shipping, of which it recovers only about 55 percent.[26] Due to its profits in other areas, Amazon can sustain enormous losses like this year after year. As the company is rapidly creating its own shipping fiefdom, these losses will likely turn into eventual capital through ROI down the road.

---

23 Stephan Serrano, "Top 10 Reasons (and Solutions) for Shopping Cart Abandonment," *Barilliance*, last modified August 5, 2020, https://www.barilliance.com/10-reasons-shopping-cart-abandonment/.

24 Neal Ungerleider, "Free Shipping is a Lie," *Fast Company*, last modified November 1, 2016, https://www.fastcompany.com/3061686/free-shipping-is-a-lie.

25 Amrita Khalid, "Amazon Doesn't Care About Losing Money on Delivery if It Keeps Customers Happy," Quartz, last modified October 31, 2019, https://qz.com/1739653/amazon-earnings-report-loss-related-to-delivery-costs/.

26 Ungerleider, "Free Shipping is a Lie."

How many years can your business afford massive losses to subsidize fast, free deliveries?

Although almost no other companies can rely on Amazon's economy of scale, they still have to deal with the by-product, as they inherit Amazon's customers' shipping expectations. In 2015, "almost 60 percent of online transactions included free shipping."[27] By 2018's holiday season, this figure reached 87 percent,[28] with analysts having long predicted a future in which all shipping is free.[29]

There are a handful of Amazon competitors who have made strides to make similar delivery services available to their customers. Walmart, still the leading retailer in the world, along with Target and a handful of others, have attempted to compete with Amazon on the same level of scale by offering their own free, two-day shipping services. Walmart and Target, in particular, have "countered by turning stores into fulfillment centers, offering customers next-day or even same-day pick-up and delivery options."[30] Given that back in 2012, 90 percent of all Americans [lived] within

27   Deborah Abrams Kaplan, "The Real Cost of e-Commerce Logistics," *Supply Chain Dive*, last modified June 6, 2017, https://www.supplychaindive.com/news/amazon-effect-logistics-cost-delivery/444138/.

28   "Share of e-Commerce Transactions in the United States with Free Shipping During Holiday Season from 2015 to 2018, by Week," *Statista*, last modified July 2019, https://www.statista.com/statistics/1053705/us-e-commerce-transactions-with-free-shipping-holiday-season/.

29   Kathleen Kusek, "The Future of Retail is Fast, Free Delivery," *Forbes*, last modified May 14, 2016, https://www.forbes.com/sites/kathleenkusek/2016/05/14/walmart-tries-to-capture-iwwiwwiwi-shoppers-with-free-delivery/#24dc8fa71ae5.

Anna Kegler, "The Psychology of Free Shipping: Why it Works as a Marketing Tool," *RJMetrics*, last modified July 14, 2014, https://blog.rjmetrics.com/2014/07/14/the-psychology-of-free-shipping-why-it-works-as-a-marketing-tool/.

30   "Walmart Statistics and Facts," Market.us, accessed September 21, 2020, https://market.us/statistics/e-commerce-websites/walmart/.

15 miles of a Walmart,"[31] this merging of online and offline sales will undoubtedly further speed delivery times and, consequently, increase the pressures on independent merchants to meet the same standards with fewer resources.

Finally, the largest indicator for other retailers, small and large, that shipping is quite possibly the key to business growth is in tracking Amazon's meteoric rise. In 2016, "some 95 percent of US consumers shopped at one of Walmart's 4,700 stores or on its website in 2016." That same year, some "42 percent of consumers spent money on Amazon," with the company "barely squeaking into the top 20" of American retailers.[32] By 2019, Amazon—mostly due to Prime's increasingly enticing offerings, in particular around shipping—had become the second-largest retailer in the country, still second only to Walmart.[33]

To survive, you've got to have everything from bikes to burritos (and Origami paper, apparently) delivered fast and free, or even the kids will complain. So, how should retailers, manufacturers, and distributors react to strategic moves which have been designed to be virtually unreproducible? The Big 5 take copying seriously and use their cash and order volumes as a strategic weapon to ensure you can't copy them. So should you spend time figuring out how to match delivery times, or should you be more worried about these giants copying little ole you?

31 "Walmart Statistics and Facts," Market.us, accessed September 21, 2020, https://market.us/statistics/e-commerce-websites/walmart/.

32 Krystina Gustafson, "Nearly Every American Spent Money at Wal-Mart Last Year," *CNBC*, last modified April 12, 2017, https://www.cnbc.com/2017/04/12/nearly-every-american-spent-money-at-wal-mart-last-year.html.

33 "Top 100 Retailers 2019," *NRF: National Retail Federation*, accessed October 11, 2020, https://nrf.com/resources/top-retailers/top-100-retailers/top-100-retailers-2019.

CHAPTER 3

THE COPYCATS

MARKETPLACE COUNTERFEITING

In 2003, Rain Design, a San Francisco-based company, launched the iGo desk, built to make interaction with the iMac more ergonomically and aesthetically appealing.[34] By the early 2010s, Rain Design had expanded into a suite of similar products, including the mStand, an aluminum stand for laptops that would, according to the company's copy, "[transform] your notebook into a stylish and stable workstation so you can work comfortably and safely all day." As *The New Yorker* reports, the stand became an "unexpected bestseller on Amazon," and not long after, "Amazon then released its own stand, with a nearly identical design, under the brand AmazonBasics, at half the price. Rain Design's sales fell."[35]

Though a recent article in *The Wall Street Journal* documents Amazon's unfair collection and use of data to compete with its own vendors, Rain Design's and others' experiences suggest that the marketplace giant has been copying its third-party sellers

---

34 "About Us," Rain Design, accessed October 11, 2020, https://www.raindesigninc.com/about.html.

35 Charles Duhigg, "Is Amazon Unstoppable?" *The New Yorker*, last modified October 10, 2019, https://www.newyorker.com/magazine/2019/10/21/is-amazon-unstoppable.

for some time. In 2017, Amazon began selling a low-backed, mid-century modern chair called the Orb, a nearly identical product to Williams Sonoma's chair of the same name. Williams Sonoma took Amazon to court, where a judge "denied Amazon's motion to dismiss the case, ruling that the company might be 'cultivating the incorrect impression' that ersatz products were authorized by Williams Sonoma."[36]

Counterfeiting has long been an issue on Amazon, as well as on the other big e-commerce marketplaces, but it is somewhat more surprising to know that Amazon itself is engaged in this form of infringement. Not just surprising, but in direct violation of its own policies, and perhaps in violation of antitrust laws as well. After stating before Congress that "when [Amazon] makes and sells its own products, it doesn't use information it collects from the site's individual third-party sellers—data those sellers view as proprietary."[37] *The WSJ* found evidence directly to the contrary. Concerning a "bestselling car-trunk organizer sold by a third-party vendor," Amazon collected documents and data, including "total sales, how much the vendor paid Amazon for marketing and shipping, and how much Amazon made on each sale. Amazon's private-label arm later introduced its own car-trunk organizers." Though Amazon claims that all of its data is aggregate and not the result of harvesting any one company's information, more than half of over 1,000 Amazon Marketplace sellers recently surveyed report that "Amazon sells its own products that directly compete with the seller's products."[38]

---

36 Ibid.

37 Dana Mattioli, "Amazon Scooped Up Data From Its Own Sellers to Launch Competing Products," *The Wall Street Journal*, last modified April 23, 2020, https://www.wsj.com/articles/amazon-scooped-up-data-from-its-own-sellers-to-launch-competing-products-11587650015?mod=hp_lead_pos2.

38 Ibid.

As it stands, Amazon's "private-label business encompasses more than forty-five brands with some 243,000 products, from AmazonBasics batteries to Stone & Beam furniture." Those brands currently account for 1 percent of its $158 billion in annual retail sales, while the company's goal is for them to account for 10 percent of retail sales by 2022.[39] It is safe to assume that no product or company is immune to this type of copying. Independent sellers must put strategic measures in place.

Unfortunately, sellers have few alternatives or realistic methods of recourse because "39 percent of US online shopping occurs on Amazon." (See section on Amazon's US e-commerce Market Share below) So not only do many brands "feel they can't afford *not* to sell on the platform,"[40] this spine-chilling feeling can come to take on urgency, as was the case with Birkenstock. The 245-year-old company, which produces handmade sandals, with thirty-two workers [touching] every pair,[41] seems like it would be particularly hard to successfully copy. When David Kahan became CEO of Birkenstock Americas, he found that "numerous companies were selling counterfeit or unauthorized Birkenstocks on Amazon; many were using fulfillment by Amazon to ship their products, which caused them to appear prominently in search results." When Kahan asked the company to remove these listings, he discovered something even more unsettling: Amazon itself "had started buying enormous numbers of Birkenstocks to resell on the site. The company had amassed more than a year's worth of inventory."[42]

---

39 Ibid.

40 Ibid.

41 Charles Duhigg, "Is Amazon Unstoppable?" *The New Yorker*, last modified October 10, 2019, https://www.newyorker.com/magazine/2019/10/21/is-amazon-unstoppable.

42 Ibid.

AMAZON'S US E-COMMERCE MARKET SHARE

Amazon's US e-commerce market share is not a straightforward figure. For one thing, the data the company offers about itself is less than clear: though we might, for example, know Amazon's total yearly revenue, it's not always known how that number breaks down across its different sectors. This is particularly problematic in creating e-commerce figures, as increasingly large chunks of Amazon's revenue come from non-e-commerce sources, such as AWS, Whole Foods, advertising, seller fees, etc. This was precisely the problem with the "50 percent of US e-commerce" headlines from 2019—this percentage used the revenue generated by Amazon as a first-person seller, as well as the fees it collected from its third-party sellers.[43] As the company was in the midst of antitrust scrutiny, Amazon clarified its revenue streams, which—as fee revenue is not consumer spending—forced analysts to drop the number considerably, to 38 percent.[44]

In as careful a consideration of Amazon's numbers as the still somewhat hazy data will allow, the analyst Benedict Evans argues that excluding all international commerce, electronic or otherwise, as well as all non-e-commerce revenue in the US, Amazon has 15 percent of the market as a first-party seller. When including all third-party sales—58 percent of all Amazon e-commerce transactions—this market share increases by

---

43 Sujay Seetharaman, "The Story of Amazon's Market Share," *PipeCandy*, last modified October 30, 2019, https://blog.pipecandy.com/amazon-market-share/.

44 Matthew Day and Spencer Soper, "Amazon U.S. Online Market Share Estimate Cut to 38% From 47%," *Bloomberg Quint*, last modified June 14, 2019, https://www.bloombergquint.com/business/emarketer-cuts-estimate-of-amazon-s-u-s-online-market-share.

some twenty points, to 35 percent.[45] Given a five-point margin, it is fair to say that Amazon's share of US e-commerce is 35 to 40 percent.

As Kahan told *The New Yorker*, "That was terrifying, because it meant we could totally lose control of our brand. What if Amazon decides to start selling the shoes for ninety-nine cents, or to give them away with Prime membership, or do a buy-one-get-one-free campaign? It would completely destroy how people see our shoes, and our only power to prevent something like that is to cut off a retailer's supply. But Amazon had a year's worth of inventory. We were powerless."[46]

Eventually, Kahan tried, unsuccessfully, to sever Birkenstock's relationship with Amazon. The shoes, often counterfeit versions for which the company's customer service team remains answerable, are still sold on Amazon at prices far below what Birkenstock requires its retailers to charge. As Kahan said, "When there's only one marketplace, and it's impossible to walk away, everything is out of balance. Amazon owns the marketplace. They can do whatever they want. That's not capitalism. That's piracy."[47]

The evidence seems to suggest that digital marketplaces like Amazon are intentionally designed to undermine participants for the benefit of the platform. As these issues are increasingly brought to court, companies are left between a rock and a hard place. Do you sell on the marketplace that may use your data and customer list to become a direct competitor, or do you risk going

45 Benedict Evans, "What's Amazon's Market Share?" *Benedict Evans*, last modified December 19, 2019, https://www.ben-evans.com/benedictevans/2019/12/amazons-market-share19.

46 Charles Duhigg, "Is Amazon Unstoppable?" *The New Yorker*, last modified October 10, 2019, https://www.newyorker.com/magazine/2019/10/21/is-amazon-unstoppable.

47 Ibid.

rogue, refusing to participate in the scheme, and possibly go out of business anyway? In the meantime, it is clear that in order to survive online, companies must not only bring great products to market, they must also make themselves, or some aspect of their business, inimitable. While Rain Design, for example, continues to be in business, other small retailers have not been as resilient. As we will see, being inimitable often requires innovation in many different areas.

CHAPTER 4

THE E-COMMERCE DATASET ADVANTAGE

Have you noticed your Amazon confirmation emails lately? The line-item details of your order have disappeared. To see the contents of your order, you have to log in to your account. Gone are the days of straightforward email summaries.

This subtle change is a sign of a full-scale data war being played out behind the scenes.

One of the long-standing battles in my house is between one of my boys, who is building a new LEGO set, and his brother, who wants to get an early view of the build. "Stop looking at my creation!" one will scream as if he's been assaulted by the peeping grade-schooler. The verbal battle escalates until my wife or I intervene.

Since this seven-year-old can't handle anyone seeing his work, it's not hard to picture Amazon seeing competitors as a threat in the battle for purchase intent data. Amazon seems to have removed line-item details from their order confirmation emails because those emails were sent to Gmail inboxes controlled by rival Google.

GOOGLE'S ANTI-AMAZON ALLIANCE

Back in 2017, Target and Google worked to expand their delivery partnership "from a small experiment in a handful of cities to the entire continental US."[48] This expansion made Target one of the prime retailers enabled by Google Assistant, Google's AI-powered virtual assistant. Walmart has also paired with Google to access their many voice commerce consumers, as the three monoliths' interests converge in finding ways to stop shoppers from going to Amazon first (this cuts out Google as the search middleman). This anti-Amazon alliance also includes smaller retailers in less direct ways, as Google is also helping companies build out their online presence in ways that directly compete with Amazon's.

Customer intent data is key to marketplace dominance. These datasets allow marketplaces to position the right item(s) in front of the right buyers when they predict they will be looking to make a purchase. Remember the 2012 story of the dad who discovered that Target's purchase data determined his high school daughter was pregnant before he even found out? Pregnant women have been referred to as retail's holy grail. If a retailer knows a woman is pregnant, they can serve her with ads to direct her new baby purchases to their stores. "We knew that if we could identify them in their second trimester, there's a good chance we could capture them for years," said Andrew Pole, a statistician for Target. "As soon as we get them buying diapers from us, they're going to start buying everything else too. If you're rushing through the store, looking for bottles, and you pass orange juice, you'll grab a carton.

---

48   Jason Del Rey, "Google Is Essentially Building an Anti-Amazon Alliance, and Target Is the Latest to Join," *Vox*, last modified October 12, 2017, https://www.vox.com/2017/10/12/16464132/google-target-retailers-amazon-walmart-assistant-alexa-home-echo-augmented-reality.

Oh, and there's that new DVD I want. Soon, you'll be buying cereal and paper towels from us, and keep coming back."[49]

The Big 5's scale and scope provide them with customer acquisition and retention advantages that smaller merchants cannot approach—the opportunity to put the right item in front of the right buyer. To do this requires SKU breadth and significant consumer traffic. The more data on both sides of the equation, the higher probability of a match. Independent retailers need the match and have few opportunities to gain the volume without depending on the marketplaces that are ongoing competitive threats. The Big 5 have invested heavily to get access to and control these consumer merchandising datasets. Similar to warehouse automation, independent merchants have opportunities to escape this trap, but it requires taking specific steps. One option from a company close to my team is Pantastic, who, reacting at least in part to the COVID crisis, is assembling a scaled, multicategory retailer from millions of independent merchants, be they luxury brands or second bedroom SMBs. They are working to deploy the AI strategies and fulfillment services of the retail giants on the independents' behalf and are "committed to supporting [independent] businesses, not preying on them" by way of their own private label brands.

Whether it is getting in front of a pregnant woman's purchasing plans or being more selective with marketplace partnerships so as to secure your customers' order history data, navigating these consumer merchandising AIs is imperative. The competitive threats in and out of the warehouse cannot be ignored.

---

49   Charles Duhigg, "How Companies Learn Your Secrets." *The New York Times*, last modified February 16, 2012, https://www.nytimes.com/2012/02/19/magazine/shopping-habits. html?pagewanted=1&_r=1&hp.

CHAPTER 5

THE GIANTS

MEET THE FIVE APIS OF
THE APOCALYPSE

My mom always told me to just be nice...terrible advice.

A Q&A in *Entrepreneur* magazine asked Simon Sinek, "What's the best way to view the competition?" Sinek answered, "A sure sign of a weak company is one that frets over the competition." We've all heard others instruct us to ignore the competition or to "say nice things about them."[50]

These brilliant entrepreneurs were clearly wrong when reading through the lens of the current Big 5 environment. Today's entrepreneurs can't ignore these giant competitors. We are living in the age of machine learning, artificial intelligence, trillion-dollar valuations, obtrusive data gathering, and companies that have become so big that "we cannot tell [them] apart from the govern-

---

50   Robert Scoble, quoted by Peter Economy, "20 Brilliant Quotes on Competition From Highly
     Successful Business Leaders," *Inc.*, last modified July 4, 2018, https://www.inc.com/peter-
     economy/20-brilliant-quotes-on-competition-from-highly-successful-business-leaders.html.

ment."[51] The competitive advantage of a few is so significant that it is smothering. In fact, we used to forbid such practices, but our antitrust laws are chasing (and being lobbied into submission by) these giants too.

Technology and business journalist Kara Swisher told *The Verge* that "One of Silicon Valley's biggest problems right now is its lack of competition. That big tech companies like Amazon, Apple, Facebook, and Google have become too dominant and have thus stifled competition and creativity."[52]

In many respects, because today's business leaders grew up in an ignore-the-competition world, we've been caught flat-footed. We saw these massive companies creeping up on us but didn't pay enough attention to their tactics.

The e-commerce infrastructure available to independents is behind, yes, but it is fighting to catch up, and those who aren't iterating and taking advantage of opportunities to automate will not be able to keep up with those who do.

Businesses have historically treated shipping and fulfillment as a set-it-and-forget-it function. If it works, don't fix it, right? Wrong. Because what appears to be working is, in fact, not working. Simply making deliveries on time and on budget is not enough. Remember, the bullets are flying, so the reality is that on time and on budget is going to get you killed.

---

51 Zachary Mack, "Big Tech's Problem Is Its Lack of Competition," *The Verge*, last modified June 25, 2019,https://www.theverge.com/2019/6/25/18744342/ big-tech-competition-antitrust-regulation-amazon-apple-facebook-google-kara-swisher-vergecast.

52 Ibid.

WE ARE FROM THE GOVERNMENT AND WE ARE HERE TO HELP

Several years ago, I was walking through the corridors of a Palm Springs hotel and convention center during the eTail West trade show. I remember the conversations, the banners, the names of the presentations. It was clear: Amazon's marketplace was a godsend. There were just so many eyeballs (shorthand for prospective buyers looking to buy).

Exactly twelve months later, the mood had changed. I was in the same hotel at the same conference. Once again, the message was clear: Amazon is a threat. I remember thinking, *"Wow, that happened fast."*

Still to this day, I talk to sellers who see Amazon and its peers as friends. I will tell you the same thing I tell them. Yes, the Big 5 want you to believe they are here to help, and yes, they can and do bring more business to their marketplace partners. But this is a Faustian bargain, and it comes at a steep cost.

To understand the real cost, we first must explore the visions each member of the Big 5 have for the future. We also need to be prepared to answer the same question for ourselves. What type of future do we envision for our businesses, our communities, and our families?

SHOPIFY

Shopify is not like the other members of the Big 5. This is a critical exception that must be brought to light in advance. Their power stems from successfully supporting independent merchants, not replacing them. Instead of putting Powered by Shopify logos on every website they power, Shopify founder and CEO Tobias Lütke says, "This is not a company that's going around like, 'Look at us,' these kinds of things. We want to make merchants look good...this is why it has no branding; wherever we can avoid branding, we do."[53]

As we will see, Shopify's vision of the future is very different. It is less than ideal for merchants' success and long-term viability to be reliant on one service provider. As uncomfortable as I am with trusting only one platform, in today's uncompetitive marketplace (for the little guys), it must be done, and Shopify is a clear ally. I say this as someone who believes the future we need is one where the independent business can thrive. It's one where business ownership is a powerful equalizer, reducing income inequality and empowering families and communities.

In a talk given at the Business of Software 2011, a conference for software entrepreneurs, Lütke urged people to "make sure their business is on the right side of history through code and culture," by asking, "How can we build businesses that people won't be embarrassed by in 100 years?"[54] Though what leads to embarrassment is surely subjective, it is objectively certain that Lütke is aiming to build a company that not only exists for 100 years—itself a rarity in startup culture—but one that also helps dictate what that future looks like.

According to the company's website, value creation at Shopify includes "the growth of small business, computing literacy, and

---

53 Shopify Partners, "An AMA with Shopify's Tobi Lütke (Shopify Unite 2017)," YouTube, May 24, 2017, https://www.youtube.com/watch?v=wrZiOxw0wXE.

54 Littlewood, Mark T. "How to make sure your business is on the right side of history through code & culture," March 23, 2012. Business of Software. Online, https://businessofsoftware.org/2012/05/tobias-lutke-ceo-shopify-at-business-of-software-2011-how-we-can-build-businesses-that-people-in-100-years-wont-be-embarrassed-by/.

personal development."[55] As computing literacy will create the "most prepared workforce," and personal development can be cycled back into "[building] the organization," Shopify's beliefs around value are not strictly altruistic. They do, however, have a remarkably different emphasis on the creative empowerment of the individual as being a huge boon for business.

Lütke has also spoken of the role of commerce in human history: "every time there were breakthroughs in the ways people conducted commerce, every time an innovation made commerce easier or faster, that's when civilization changed."[56] Clearly implying that Shopify could be a "part of one of those breakthroughs," it is important to note that from the consumer end, "the company is practically invisible," which allows companies' brands to be "front and centre."[57] If, as commentator Scott Galloway says, Amazon "partners with companies the way a virus partners with a host... Shopify's business model is the opposite. It's the perfect partner for brands looking to build their own business."[58]

It is fair to say that the future of commerce that Shopify envisions remains unique. As Lütke told *The Motley Fool*, "How many people do you think would want a profitable side business? Like if you would give everyone a big, red button and ask them to push it if they want one of those side businesses, literally everyone would

55 "Value Creation," Shopify, accessed October 11, 2020, https://investors.shopify.com/long-term-value/default.aspx.

56 Trevor Cole, "Our Canadian CEO of the Year You've Probably Never Heard of," *The Globe and Mail*, last modified November 27, 2014, https://www.theglobeandmail.com/report-on-business/rob-magazine/meet-our-ceo-of-the-year/article21734931/.

57 Dianne Buckner, "Canadian e-Commerce Firm Shopify Looks Set to Challenge Amazon," *CBC*, last modified October 30, 2019, https://www.cbc.ca/news/business/canadian-e-commerce-firm-shopify-looks-set-to-challenge-amazon-1.5339370.

58 Ibid.

push it, right?"[59] Not only is Shopify in their own business of creating those big, red buttons, they are also looking to e-commerce as a potential site of disruption for who gets to push them.

TENCENT/JD

Judging by Tencent's primary business as the biggest gaming company in the world, as well as the owner of the world's third-largest messaging app, WeChat—behind only WhatsApp and Facebook Messenger[60]—the company's vision of the future seems clear: it is one spent in endless screen time, a screen which is, more and more, that of the smartphone.

Though such an assessment isn't inaccurate, it also doesn't tell the whole story. As many of China's current entrepreneurs have come of age under their then leader Deng Xiaoping's famous "Opening of China," begun in the late 1970s, businesses in China have been in the unique position of helping shape the very economic structures in which they participate (consider, for instance, retail holding almost double the gross domestic product (GDP) in China as it does in the US[61]).[62] As Pony Ma, Tencent's founder, has said, the digital economy "could become the engine driving the next phase

59 "Interview With Shopify CEO Tobias Lutke," *The Motley Fool*, last modified August 15, 2019, https://www.fool.com/investing/2019/08/15/interview-with-shopify-ceo-tobias-lutke.aspx.

60 Birgit Bucher, "WhatsApp, WeChat and Facebook Messenger Apps—Global Messenger Usage, Penetration and Statistics," *messengerpeople*, last modified February 12, 2020, https://www.messengerpeople.com/global-messenger-usage-statistics/.

61 Adam Lashinksy, "Alibaba v. Tencent: The Battle for Supremacy in China," *Fortune*, last modified June 21, 2018,https://fortune.com/longform/alibaba-tencent-china-internet/.

62 Abraham Denmark, "40 Years Ago, Deng Xiaoping Changed China—and the World," *The Washing Post*, last modified December 19, 2018, https://www.washingtonpost.com/news/monkey-cage/wp/2018/12/19/40-years-ago-deng-xiaoping-changed-china-and-the-world/.

of growth."[63] Recognizing this possibility has informed Tencent's investment strategy, which "[leans] more towards backing [partners] strategically instead of holding controlling shares directly." This "little fingers in many pies" approach as led the company to create an environment in which partners are "[supported and empowered] to success."[64]

Along with Snap and Tesla, and not so coincidentally Walmart and Google, one such investment has been into JD.com. With Tencent's partnership, JD has gained entry to the WeChat ecosystem and its one billion-plus users. As analysts have pointed out, Tencent and Alibaba have created "'walled-garden' versions of the internet," in which, says digital strategy consultant, Tom Birtwhistle, "consumers are blocked from traversing the two internets," such that users can't "move easily, for instance, from WeChat to Taobao."[65] Thus, though JD, as discussed elsewhere, is building similarly to Amazon, by aligning itself with Tencent, JD is already much closer to Bezos' vision of becoming the market itself, as the primary e-commerce provider for its walled-garden version of the internet. When you couple this with all of the data Tencent has been mining for years through its games and apps, Pony Ma's digital economy of the future begins to take shape, and it's one in which JD looms large.

63 He Wei, Cheng Yu, and Liu Yukun, "Pony Ma Shares His Vision for Business," *China Daily*, last modified March 13, 2018, http://www.chinadaily.com.cn/a/201803/13/WS5aa739dfa3106e7dcc1414eb.html.

64 Ibid.

65 Adam Lashinsky, "Alibaba v. Tencent: The Battle for Supremacy in China." *Fortune*, last modified June 21, 2018, https://fortune.com/longform/alibaba-tencent-china-internet/.

JD AND HUGGIES

Data collection allows companies to monetize information in ways beyond just targeted ads—consider, for example, US diaper brand, Huggies. JD.com helped Huggies figure out "why Chinese competitors were rising in popularity," prompting the diaper makers to "change to a material that is more absorbent and comfortable when wet. That contributed to a 60 percent rise in Huggies sales in 2018..."[66]

ALIBABA

Perhaps more than any other Big 5 founder, Alibaba's Jack Ma has stringently associated himself and his businesses with a future mindset. The 2017 compilation of his thoughts is, after all, subtitled *The Future Has Come*. When he retired from Alibaba in 2019 on his fifty-fifth birthday, Ma announced his intentions to "[improve] education through philanthropy," stating that he would rather "appropriate the earnings he's made from Alibaba to positively changing the education system in China, instead of handing it to investors or banks."[67] Many, however, have speculated that his move wasn't altogether selfless, with *The Washington Post* reporting that "prominent Chinese entrepreneurs who receive press attention are more likely to be investigated or arrested compared to those who shy away from media coverage."[68] As Ma has

66 Cate Cadell and Pei Li, "Data 'R' Us: Alibaba, JD.com Seek to Lock in Merchant Loyalty with New Services," *Reuters*, last modified June 20, 2019, https://www.reuters.com/article/us-china-tech-retail/data-r-us-alibaba-jd-com-seek-to-lock-in-merchant-loyalty-with-new-services-idUSKCN1TL09D.

67 Jack Kelly, "From Poor Beginnings to Billionaire Status: Jack Ma Retires From Alibaba." *Forbes*, last modified September 10, 2019, https://www.forbes.com/sites/jackkelly/2019/09/10/from-poor-beginnings-to-billionaire-status-jack-ma-retires-from-alibaba/#675301ebd29a.

68 Ibid.

definitely been in the former camp throughout his career, such a transition appears to be yet another future-prudent move.

This awareness of his cultural and political circumstances, and the boundaries of either, has marked Ma and Alibaba's colossal success. In conversation with Aki Anastasiou, host of Eyewitness News' *Technobyte*, about the future of Africa, Ma said that he was reminded of himself twenty years ago in China: "Entrepreneurs have to think differently...E-commerce is designed for developing countries. E-commerce is designed for small business, not for big companies."[69] Speaking elsewhere, Ma said that his "ambition is to enable two billion young people to be able to do business whenever you want as long as you have a mobile phone."[70]

Recognizing e-commerce's potential in developing countries and emerging global economies has surely helped pave Ma's path. At the same time—perhaps taking his own assessment of e-commerce and big companies to heart—Alibaba has understood that it must innovate in order to succeed. Like WeChat, Alibaba is seeking to combine online and offline retail through its "New Retail," which "aims to digitize the retail experience for its consumers." The *Economic Times* wrote that Alibaba's "New Retail" is "the driving force behind the rising trend of digitising supermarkets, hospitality, and retail stores." Writing to shareholders, Ma spoke of Alibaba's "re-imagined retail industry: "[O]ver the next 30 years, with computing power as the new 'technology breakthrough' and data as the new 'natural resource,' the landscape of retail, financial services, manufacturing, and entertainment will

---

69 Eyewitness News, "Jack Ma: Africa Is the Future," YouTube, August 12, 2018, https://www.youtube.com/watch?v=9stffnthTGQ.

70 CCTV English, "How Alibaba CEO Jack Ma Transformed the e-Commerce Industry," YouTube, September 1, 2019, https://www.youtube.com/watch?v=xJ4QoygrrKE.

be transformed."[71] Given what Alibaba has managed to do in the last twenty years, Ma's vision of the future seems more than likely.

WALMART

Of the Big 5, Walmart is the only nondigital native; its beginnings are far removed from e-commerce. If Alibaba, Tencent, and Amazon are recognizing that the future of retail involves an online-offline hybrid (Alibaba's "New Retail," for example), and are thus looking for ways to expand into and transform the brick-and-mortar world, Walmart's trajectory comes from the opposite direction, as it seeks to translate its staggering physical presence into the virtual realm.

As many have noted, this translation hasn't been altogether fluent. Though Walmart changed the nature of retail to such a degree that there's an entire "effect" named after it. The so-called "Walmart Effect" includes the "driving down of local prices for all everyday necessities, the draining of the viability of the traditional local shopping areas, a continual downward pressure on local wages, [and] the consolidation of consumer product companies aiming to match Walmart's scale"[72]. Walmart seems to have trouble innovating around this latest retail phase change. As *The Motley Fool* stated, "Walmart was reluctant to make the necessary investments and absorb the losses required to match Amazon, which ran its e-commerce business at breakeven for much of its history."[73]

---

71   Poorabi Gaekwad, "Open Sesame: A Look into Alibaba's Vision for the Vuture," *The Economic Times*, last modified September 26, 2019, https://economictimes.indiatimes.com/tech/internet/open-sesame-a-look-into-alibabas-vision-for-the-future/articleshow/71295105.cms?from=mdr.

72   "The Wal-Mart Effect," Wikipedia, accessed November 16, 2019, https://en.wikipedia.org/wiki/The_Wal-Mart_Effect.

73   Jeremy Bowman, "Is Walmart's E-Commerce Strategy Failing?" *The Motley Fool*, last modified February 15, 2020, https://www.fool.com/investing/2020/02/15/is-walmarts-e-commerce-strategy-failing.aspx.

In 2016, Walmart "agreed to the largest-ever acquisition of an e-commerce company: a $3.3 billion purchase of a fast-growing but money-sucking online shopping site called Jet.com."[74] Many analysts figured that a part of this astonishing sum was Walmart paying for the pleasure of employing Marc Lore in its e-commerce sector. Nonetheless, aside from its online grocery division—something with which Lore has no part—Walmart has continued to bleed money. *The Wall Street Journal* estimates that "US online operations lost around $2 billion" in the 2018–19 fiscal year.[75]

These losses come despite increased online sales under Lore's guidance, and Walmart began investing heavily in its e-commerce future by building fulfillment warehouses and acquiring new, exciting brands. For a "company obsessed with frugality that finely calibrates its financial goals"[76]—an obsession directly at odds with both startup and Amazon cultures, which are far more comfortable with heavy losses for future gains—such losses have been largely unacceptable. In May of 2020, amidst a 74 percent spike in US e-commerce sales due to the pandemic, Walmart announced that it would be discontinuing Jet. Instead, the company would dedicate its efforts more fully to Walmart.com, including testing a two-hour delivery service.[77] At the same time, Walmart continues to try to cut its losses by "shifting the focus from an Amazon-style model of fulfillment warehouses to giant stores, which serve a

74 Jason Del Rey, "Inside the Conflict at Walmart that's Threatening its High-Stakes Race with Amazon," *Vox*, last modified July 3, 2019, https://www.vox.com/recode/2019/7/3/18716431/walmart-jet-marc-lore-modcloth-amazon-e-commerce-losses-online-sales.

75 Sarah Nassauer, "Walmart's Secret Weapon to Fight Off Amazon: The Supercenter," *The Wall Street Journal*, last modified December 21, 2019, https://www.wsj.com/articles/walmarts-secret-weapon-to-fight-off-amazon-the-supercenter-11576904460.

76 Ibid.

77 Ingrid Lunden, "Walmart Says It Will Discontinue Jet, Which It Acquired for $3B in 2016," *TechCrunch*, last modified May 19, 2020, https://techcrunch.com/2020/05/19/walmart-says-it-will-discontinue-jet-com-which-it-acquired-for-3b-in-2016/.

double purpose both to push its brick-and-mortar strategy, and to serve as the fulfillment hubs for the online-facing part of its business."[78]

As the company itself hasn't seemed to figure it out, it is difficult to say what Walmart's future vision for e-commerce is. Not only did Walmart end Jet.com a mere four years after acquiring it, it also shut down its online grocery app, folding it into the larger Walmart app.[79] Its tremendous existing retail presence—still the largest in the world—ensures their ongoing place in any conversation, but as a success story or cautionary tale remains to be seen.

AMAZON

So much of this book will speak of warehousing and e-commerce in relation to Amazon that an aside for the company's vision of the future might seem redundant. Those of us in America are far more experientially familiar with Amazon and its dominance than with, say, WeChat's. Knowing as we do some aspects of the "Amazon future"—voice-placed orders delivered via drone to consumers wherever their phone geolocates them—it is still nevertheless clarifying to place Amazon's goals in relation to the rest of the Big 5.

When Jack Ma speaks of e-commerce as designed for developing countries, he is speaking to something inherently similar to Tobi Lütke's "red button." In an ideal, or perhaps even utopian situation, the internet is an equalizer. It grants entry and access to those who have long been denied, be it from freedom of speech or

78 Ibid.

79 Hayley Peterson, "Walmart Is Killing Off Its Most Popular App as Online Shopping Reaches Record Highs—and It's a Brilliant Strategy," *Business Insider*, last modified May 20, 2020, https://www.businessinsider.com/walmart-kills-grocery-app-to-make-online-shopping-easier-2020-5.

commerce. Ant Group, a subsidiary of Alibaba, created Sesame Credit—an "alternative to traditional credit scores"—along these lines, or at least claimed to.[80] By "[broadening] access to loans in a developing market by monitoring people's buying habits and social circles as well as their credit records," the intention was to make commercial life "easier for those on the margin."[81] In an emerging economy in which huge portions of the population don't have financial records or relationships with banks, such an idea is surely innovative and intriguing.

Though Amazon and Alibaba find themselves in more similar positions in the global market than not, their starting positions were vastly different. (The social credit system currently used in China that stems from ideas akin to Sesame Credit is far more about control and surveillance than equal access.) As e-commerce and consumerism in general had relatively simultaneous introductions to the Chinese population than to the American public, Amazon's task has been to shift the brick-and-mortar consumer towards e-commerce. Amazon has, as commentators frequently point out, fundamentally changed how we shop. It has done this through one-click, through Prime, through Alexa, through two-day, same-day, two-hour shipping—the list goes on and on.

Rather than repeat what I say throughout this book about Amazon's desire to become the marketplace itself—the everything store with limitless digital aisles—I'd like to consider instead the consumer that Amazon has created. That consumer is hooked on speed and convenience, and, though the change may seem sudden, it is one that has been in the works for some time. "Amazon has been influencing consumer buying behaviors since 1994, allowing

80 John Gapper, "Alibaba's Social Credit Rating Is a Risky Game," *Financial Times*, last modified February 20, 2018, https://www.ft.com/content/99165d7a-1646-11e8-9376-4a6390addb44.

81 Ibid.

the company to affect an entire generation of purchasing deci-sions."[82] The consumers behind those purchasing decisions have been willing to overlook labor code violations, environmental deg-radation, and general ruthlessness (one of Amazon's alternative names was, after all, Relentless.com[83]). Just as we need to ask ourselves what kind of commerce future we want for ourselves and our communities, we also need to ask what kind of consumers we want to be.

---

82 Jennifer Flanagan, "6 Ways Amazon Has Changed Buying Behaviors," *Total Retail*, last modified September 12, 2018, https://www.mytotalretail.com/ article/6-ways-amazon-has-changed-buying-behaviors/.

83 Dave Smith, "Jeff Bezos almost gave Amazon a different name," *Business Insider*, last modified January 22, 2016, https://www.businessinsider.com/jeff-bezos-amazon-name-alternatives-2016-1.

PART 2

WAREHOUSES, MONEY, AND ROBOTS, OH MY

CHAPTER 6

WAREHOUSE AUTOMATION

YOUR SECRET WEAPON

The online British grocery retailer, Ocado, describes itself as an "online grocery technology pioneer." The company started life as an automation-first retailer with no physical stores—just highly automated CFC's (customer fulfillment centers) that form part of an intelligent, end-to-end e-commerce, fulfillment, and logistics platform. Because they have no physical stores, orders are placed via Apple and Android apps, the Apple Watch, and even voice commands via Amazon's Alexa. Orders are fulfilled with home delivery services from regional, centralized sites using thousands of robots and artificial intelligence in order, according to the company, to "plan and optimize picking sequence, product location, and crate routing" to the pick station, which brings pick times of a fifty-item grocery order down to just five minutes. All of Ocado's technology is developed in-house. At Erith, their largest UK warehouse, engineers have installed several robotic "suction cup" picking stations, which use computer vision to transfer an item from its crate into the customer's bag. The company is also doing R&D into a "soft manipulation" robot that would be able to pick up delicate objects, like, say, bananas, without crushing them.

A robotic arm with "soft rubber fingers filled with pressurized air" would grasp many different objects delicately, as *The Verge* reports, and would be able to hoist a bag of limes without making juice.[84]

All aspects of this process—from the website where a customer orders a bag of limes, to the multiple, behind-the-scenes software systems that transmit orders and calculate the closest distribution center with available product (to the order documents, to the robot with the soft rubber fingers attempting to grasp the limes without crushing them, to the calculation of what type and quantity of packaging to use, to the most appropriate shipping carrier and service...you get the point!)—all of these (and more) fall under the umbrella of the ever-widening industry of warehouse automation. I know, it's a literal mouthful and not getting simpler anytime soon, and in this way, automation—intended to clarify and streamline companies' work and product flows—has itself become a multipiece monster whose complexities are daunting to consider.

One would think by now that warehouse automation would be well understood and opportunities would be well documented and, in many cases, standardized. But this is not how this market has evolved. The truth is, warehouse automation is big, complex, and messy. While many supply chain professionals read news of the latest automation advancements, they go to work afraid of disrupting legacy software systems and carrier relationships. They are comfortable with some components but fail to understand the goals that should be put in place, the right order for making change, or the measurements that should be used to monitor progress.

Nine out of ten prospects that my sales team speaks to don't even

---

84   James Vincent, "Welcome to the Automated Warehouse of the Future," *The Verge,* last modified May 8, 2018, https://www.theverge.com/2018/5/8/17331250/automated-warehouses-jobs-ocado-andover-amazon. Accessed March 2020.

have shipping or fulfillment goals in place, nor do they have consistently reported metrics by which to measure progress. As my dad would say, "More is not a number." Instead, businesses routinely hire consultants who have specialized knowledge or seasoned ops leaders who they hope will be able to put their past experience to work in a new, very different operation. To be clear, some do. A handful of these leaders really know their stuff. Although what we see most frequently is different warehouses, located in the same or similar regions, fulfilling the same products to similar customer demographics, and each of them is employing a completely different workflow, while all of them claim theirs is "the best" or "the most efficient."

Before we can put the pieces of this large complex problem together, we need to start with the basics.

HARDWARE, NOT ROBOTS

Warehouse automations are not new. Take, for instance, the barcode scanner. The barcode, believe it or not, has been with us since 1951, but it didn't come into widespread use until supermarkets adopted the technology in 1973. The first scanned item was a pack of Wrigley's chewing gum in 1974.[85] The barcode is one of the most basic components of warehouse automation, and its use enables many different data points to be stored, accessed, and analyzed, either remotely or on-site. Barcodes, like all other automation efforts, aim to minimize repetition and the possibility of human error.

(01)95012345678903(3103)000123

---

85 "Barcode," Wikipedia, accessed May 6, 2020, https://en.wikipedia.org/wiki/Barcode.

The benefits of automation are as simple as a barcode scanner, and it far exceeds simple efficiencies and error reductions. Many of today's operations teams use tools like these to perform what were, just a few short years ago, extraordinary feats, processing hundreds, thousands, or even tens of thousands of orders a day with limited, yet still crucial human involvement.

Building upon the systems enabled by barcode labeling, warehouse automation has become an industry unto itself. This is not surprising! As the *Supply Chain Management Review* has said, "Warehouse automation is one of the last areas where long-term costs can be significantly reduced."[86] Among its main benefits are: "reduced labor costs, increased operational efficiency, increased workplace safety, and the ability to address labor availability concerns."[87] In its vastness, automation can mean algorithms used for warehouse space maximization, just as it can mean the design and use of increasingly sophisticated robotics used in both picking and packing shipments.

Warehouse automation takes various forms, but the goals are usually the same—reduce costs, improve throughput, rinse and repeat. At times, but not often enough, teams are also looking to integrate sustainability measures, or they want to improve the work environment for their warehouse workers, but cost savings and speed of service drive most of the change.

Warehouse automation tools and processes not only make businesses more competitive in a world where the competition can

---

86 Charlie Tanner, "Warehouse Automation Buyers Guide," *Supply Chain Management Review*, last modified May 30, 2015, https://www.scmr.com/article/warehouse_automation_buyers_guide.

87 "The Supply Chain Professional's Guide to Warehouse Automation," Conveyco, accessed October 11, 2020, https://www.conveyco.com/warehouse-automation-guide/.

invest $200 million in a new distribution center,[88] they also make the productivity of warehouse workers appear superhuman, although not without a human downside, which we will discuss in detail.

HOW WAREHOUSE AUTOMATION KEEPS SHIPPERS COMPETITIVE

We tactically defined the breadth of warehouse automation in the previous section, but a tactical understanding is not enough. It's important to detail the direct benefits companies should seek to gain—and be prepared to measure—by putting these systems in place.

Operations teams should look at automation to:

1. Reduce operations costs
   A. **Reduce labor costs.** Operations processes like managing inventory, item picking, and order fulfillment are labor-intensive. Much of this work can be augmented with automation hardware and software. On average, labor costs make up "65 percent of most warehouse facilities' operating budgets," a percentage that surpasses the "costs associated with taxes, utilities, rent (or building maintenance), and distribution combined."[89] While labor is an undeniably crucial aspect of warehouse operations, "almost 20 percent of warehouse workers responding to a recent Gallup poll describe themselves as "actively disen-

---

88   "Amazon Invests Another $1.8 Million for Raleigh Project," *ABC Local 24*, last modified February 26, 2020, https://www.localmemphis.com/article/money/business/local-business/amazon-drops-another-1-8-million-for-raleigh-project/522-4d4e9e11-90ec-417c-8039-71ec28586e93.

89   Ed Romaine, "20 Warehouse Automation Statistics That'll Blow Your Mind," Conveyco, last modified May 21, 2018, https://www.conveyco.com/warehouse-automation-statistics/.

gaged" from their work.[90] As many as half of those surveyed were doing just enough work to get by." As Pat Kelley, CEO of Labor Development Group says, "Warehouse quality and efficiency cannot be at their peak when so valuable a resource is so poorly applied to the task at hand."[91]

B. **Reduce shipping costs.** Carrier tariffs (the rates and rules under which a shipping carrier will transport goods) are complex by design. Today's tariffs are too complicated for human management and decision-making. Significant cost reductions can be realized by using software to automate carrier and service selection. Companies that are unable to work out the often-labyrinthine complexities behind shipping rules and regulations can pay as much as 40 percent in fees[92] and possible increases of up to 25 percent.[93]

2. Improve space utilization

A. **Improve order throughput and inventory turnover.** The speed at which a business can sell inventory is a crucial measure of overall health. The drag created by slow order fulfillment times means inventory sits on the shelf longer, reducing inventory turnover rates. With the number and variety of products handled by companies steadily increasing, by 2018, "the average number of SKUs in a warehouse reached 13,985," of which roughly 43 percent could be handled robotically.[94] With the number two issue for ware-

90 Lisa Harrington, "Warehouse Labor Performance: And the Winner is...Everyone," Inbound Logistics, last modified May 1, 2008, https://www.inboundlogistics.com/cms/article/warehouse-labor-performance-and-the-winner-iseveryone/.

91 Ibid.

92 "Is Your Business Overspending on Shipping?" *LateShipment*, accessed October 11, 2020, https://www.lateshipment.com/blog/is-your-business-overspending-on-shipping/.

93 "Understanding FedEx Dimensional Weight Pricing," *Shipware*, last modified April 5, 2019, https://shipware.com/blog/understanding-fedex-dimensional-weight-pricing/.

94 John Gomez, "50 Warehouse Automation Stats You Should Know," 6 River Systems, last modified August 28, 2020, https://6river.com/warehouse-automation-statistics/.

house and distribution centers being insufficient space,[95] automation helps operations know what and where merchandise is. In addition to an average 25 percent gain in overall productivity, moving to a WMS from paper-based systems leads to "a 10-20 percent improvement in space utilization, and a 15-30 percent reduction in safety stock."[96]

B. **Increase inventory storage density.** Pallet racking systems (single deep vs. double deep) improve storage density and lower overall storage costs. As all aspects of warehouse operations operate in a feedback loop with one another, assessing different automated storage systems can result in reductions in "labor, management, transportation, energy, and maintenance costs."[97]

C. **Improve inventory accuracy.** Simply knowing what is in stock can be an uphill battle for pen-and-paper operations. Automation can improve picking efficiencies. "Pick-to-Light, RFID, and Pick-to-Voice technologies reduce picking error rates by 67 percent," and improve product order and receiving accuracy. Automated storage and retrieval systems (AS/RS) have the potential to increase order accuracy levels to above 99.99 percent,"[98] and reduce theft by knowing what and where your inventory is.

D. **Optimize order fulfillment.** With automation, picking accuracy and speed, carton and packaging selection, packing efficiency, order composition, ship-from automation, back orders, and overall order fulfillment speed

95 Ibid.

96 Ibid.

97 Elliot Maras, "Inventory Costs Drive Need For Greater Storage Density," Food Logistics, last modified October 16, 2015, https://www.foodlogistics.com/3pl-4pl/article/12118974/inventory-costs-drive-need-for-greater-storage-density.

98 Ed Romaine, "20 Warehouse Automation Statistics That'll Blow Your Mind," Conveyco, last modified May 21, 2018, https://www.conveyco.com/warehouse-automation-statistics/.

are all streamlined. Seeing as employees can spend "more than 50 percent of picking time" walking through a warehouse,[99] sortation systems, for example, can "reduce the time your workers spend walking each day by up to 40 percent, increasing the picker's time per order, reducing labor hours, and allowing you to move workers to other areas of higher-value work."[100]

E. **Customize workflows.** Control over workflows for changes on the fly due to inventory types, ship-from optimizations, and buying-pattern changes are increasingly sought after. The importance and usefulness of customizable workflows in a crisis situation like COVID can be extrapolated down to more mundane changes in business. Leading the curve, Fetch Robotics recently announced Workflow Builder, which "provides a visual and intuitive tool that customers can use to deploy flexible automation in days, iterate to perfect workflows, change workflows as needs evolve, and later integrate into WMS (warehouse management systems), WES (warehouse execution systems), or fixed automation, and do all of this in-house without having to rely on third-party resources."[101]

F. **Ensure warehouse safety.** Hardware investments can move products to employees instead of moving employees to products, resulting in reduced lifting, carrying, and other areas that can cause frequent injury. Because the warehouse worker's "fatal injury rate…is higher than the

---

99   "Warehouse Automation Stats: Six Numbers You Can't Ignore," inVia Robotics, accessed October 11, 2020, https://www.inviarobotics.com/blog/warehouse-automation-stats-six-numbers-you-cant-ignore/.

100 Raymond Cocozza, "How Sortation Can Optimize Your Pick System," Conveyco, last modified May 4, 2017, https://www.conveyco.com/sortation-can-benefit-pick-system/.

101 "Fetch Robotics Launches Workflow Builder to Provide Instant Warehouse Automation," *Cision PR Newswire*, last modified March 2, 2020, https://www.prnewswire.com/news-releases/fetch-robotics-launches-workflow-builder-to-provide-instant-warehouse-automation-301013992.html.

national average for employees in all sectors,"[102] these improvements are literally lifesaving. Automation—from "conveyors and automated guided vehicles" to "automated storage and retrieval systems (AS/RS)"—can help DCs "keep up with increased fulfillment demands without putting humans at risk."[103]

G. **Reduce or eliminate errors.** Mispicks and product damage can be caught before the order is shipped. Returns can be streamlined for cost reduction and high-level customer service. According to a survey done by *Robotics Business Review*, automated warehouses are "76 percent more likely to boost inventory accuracy to 99 percent or higher, 36 percent more likely to have reduced labor costs an average of 3 percent per year, and 40 percent more likely to consistently ship within one day of an order's placement."[104]

H. **Ensure environmental responsibility.** Though still demanding fast and largely free shipping, customers are also increasingly desirous that their shipments' packaging be environmentally responsible, at least to some degree.[105] This consumer demand, along with shipping practices, has a bit of catch-up to do: "about 165 billion packages are shipped in the US each year, with the cardboard used

---

102 "How Warehouse Automation Improves Employee Safety," F&A Data Systems, Incorporated, last modified November 13, 2017, http://fadata.com/industry-news/how-warehouse-automation-improves-employee-safety/.

103 Derek Rickard, "Warehouse Automation: A New Age of Workplace Safety and Efficiency," *Supply & Demand Chain Executive*, December 26, 2019, https://www.sdcexec.com/warehousing/article/21104681/warehouse-automation-a-new-age-of-workplace-safety-and-efficiency.

104 John Gomez, "50 Warehouse Automation Stats You Should Know," 6 River Systems, last modified August 28, 2020, https://6river.com/warehouse-automation-statistics/.

105 Andrew Martins, "Most Consumers Want Sustainable Products and Packaging," *Business News Daily*, last modified June 4, 2019, https://www.businessnewsdaily.com/15087-consumers-want-sustainable-products.html.

roughly equating to more than 1 billion trees."[106] Automating shipping operations can help to reduce packing material usage, pack shipments in the proper cartons to reduce overages and DIM weight charges, reduce extra carrier charges by ensuring every order is matched with the right truck, and limit returns whenever possible.

I. **Improve customer communication.** As the vast majority of consumers expect to be able to monitor their orders every step of the way, keeping customers updated throughout their entire order life cycle becomes increasingly important. (A Dropoff survey reports that "85 percent of consumers will buy from a retailer again if they can track their purchases throughout the delivery process."[107]) Post-purchase software can give customers the controls to update shipments, access replacement inventory data, and process their own returns. Some WMSs "even provide customers with automatic order updates so they can stay informed as [the shipper] prepare[s] their order for delivery."[108]

J. **Reduce labor requirements.** Hiring qualified employees is a challenge even in the best of times. In 2018, 55 percent of warehouse managers surveyed reported that labor scarcity was one of their top organizational issues.[109] Through technology and more efficient practices, warehouse auto-

106 Jon Bird, "What A Waste: Online Retail's Big Packaging Problem," *Forbes*, last modified July 29, 2018, https://www.forbes.com/sites/jonbird1/2018/07/29/what-a-waste-online-retails-big-packaging-problem/#4ad1dad6371d.

107 Jasmine Glasheen, "Is Real-Time Order Tracking Becoming Table Stakes for e-Tailers?" *RetailWire*, last modified July 9, 2018, https://retailwire.com/discussion/is-real-time-order-tracking-becoming-table-stakes-for-e-tailers/.

108 "Improve Customer Service with Warehouse Management Software," *Scanco*, Online, https://web.archive.org/web/20190910055920/https://www.scanco.com/improve-customer-service-with-warehouse-management-software/.

109 John Gomez, "50 Warehouse Automation Stats You Should Know," 6 River Systems, last modified August 28, 2020, https://6river.com/warehouse-automation-statistics/.

mation—both hardware and software—reduces reliance on headcount to get orders out the door.

The bottom line is that warehouse automation is complex; it differs based on business model, products stocked, available technologies, and is absolutely necessary to remain cost-competitive while meeting buyers' demanding expectations in today's marketplace.

To truly be competitive, operators must master six main sectors, all of which are subject to business size and stage, but no less important to small or large shippers. Let's look at these critical components.

1. Shipping
2. Packing
3. Warehousing
4. Data and Analytics
5. Robotics
6. Operations Workers

Though "automation" has inevitably been linked to the image of robots trawling vast concrete aisles, we first want to examine lesser discussed, but no less impactful aspects of automation related to packing and shipping.

CHAPTER 7

SHIPPING

"Shipping" is frequently the catchall executives use to describe a broad array of operational functions. However, the truth is, shipping is a specific lever, far from all-encompassing, and one that can yield outsized wins or losses.

The ShipHawk sales team once dove deep into the operation of an automotive parts distributor who was considering our software. The company was single-sourcing with FedEx (parcel and LTL). The COO was confused about the difference between a freight audit company, who reviews prior invoices to verify accuracy and coaches shippers through contract negotiations, and ShipHawk's software that programmatically puts shippers in control of tariff management and utilization. That confusion led to his decision to focus on tariff negotiation and not on fulfillment workflow automations prior to the peak holiday shipping period.

We touched base with the company after the turn of the year to see if we could reengage and learned that Christmas sales were fantastic, but that the COO's job was now on the line because profitability was in the toilet.

What happened?

The warehouse team at one DC mispacked a single item through-out the entire peak season. This one SKU was packed in a box that was bigger than necessary, which triggered a 2018 FedEx oversize surcharge of $300 per shipment, a fee that was increased to $675 in 2019 and $875 in 2020.[110] FedEx calls these "unauthorized package charges."[111] Put simply, FedEx will accept the shipment into its parcel network and penalize the shipper afterward. As consumers have become more comfortable purchasing large items online, like furniture and appliances, the carriers' physical infra-structures that were designed for homogenous freight types (small boxes and envelopes shipped parcel, larger items on 4x4 pallets for LTL), have become strained. As they rush to adapt physical assets, they are also aggressively working to "train" their customers by way of exorbitant fees. These also nicely pad earnings, a pricing strategy we will discuss below.

So, what happened to our automotive parts distributor? Enough of these items were purchased that this mistake—on a single SKU—ate the company's entire profit for the quarter, and they ended the holiday season in the red.

OVERSPENDING ON SHIPPING—THE BITTER TRUTH

Though not a 45 percent loss on shipping expenditure like Amazon's, most business-to-consumer entities lose some-where between 2 percent and 5 percent of net sales on shipping expenses. For example, a small retailer with net sales of $5 million is spending between $100,000 and $200,000 more on shipping

---

110 "FedEx Shipping Rates: Surcharges and Fees," FedEx, last modified September 14, 2020, https://www.fedex.com/en-us/shipping/current-rates/surcharges-and-fees.html.

111 Ibid.

than they should. A midsize retailer with $20 million in net sales is potentially losing $1 million a year on overspend. Though business-to-business entities may currently make modest positive offsets in their shipping expenses, this will change "as marketplaces push into b-to-b, [and they are forced to] offer reduced or free shipping."[112] These 2 to 5 percent losses, however, are from shipping as planned—they are, in other words, the price of doing business with customers with "Amazon expectations."

Some companies' solution to this problem of overspending on shipping is to simply push these losses to their marketing budgets, chalking it up as part of the price of acquiring customers. Pushing shipping losses into marketing, however, dramatically spikes the customer acquisition cost (CAC), it can obscure true shipping costs, and doesn't solve the baseline problem.[113]

To make matters worse, these losses do not include the costs of shipping errors, which very likely drives the true number of shipping-incurred losses much higher. From oversize charges to simply shipping an order in the wrong box, the leakage is everywhere. My company, ShipHawk, has analyzed millions of transactions in an effort to drill down on these violations. We found that carrier and service routing is one of the biggest offenders. In fact, 22.3 percent of the orders we analyzed were shipped with the wrong carrier or service. This can mean shipping an order with two-day air service, when a less expensive option will meet the delivery promise, or shipping with the wrong carrier in a multicarrier environment.

---

112 "Do You Understand Where You're Losing Money on Shipping & Handling?" F. Curtis Barry & Company, accessed October 11, 2020, https://www.fcbco.com/blog/do-you-understand-where-youre-losing-money-on-shipping-handling.

113 Michael Lewis, "The Effect of Shipping Fees on Customer Acquisition, Customer Retention, and Purchase Quantities," *Journal of Retailing* 82, no. 1 (2006): 13–23. https://doi.org/10.1016/j.jretai.2005.11.005.

Especially in the business-to-consumer realm, most shippers must also consider the unwanted but likely possibility of this entire operation happening in reverse, with consumers sending merchandise back. An easy, inexpensive return policy is frequently cited as crucial by consumers,[114] so shippers must also anticipate bearing some, if not all, of the return shipping costs. CNBC called returns a "$260 billion ticking time bomb," with return rates of "30 percent or more for merchandise that's bought online. Clothing returns can be closer to 40 percent."[115] As Tobin Moore, CEO of Optoro, says, "many retailers are getting 15 cents to 30 cents on the dollar for these returns because they're having such trouble economically processing them and getting them to the next best markets."[116] This 70 to 85 percent loss doesn't even factor in shipping costs!

In 2018, the Council of Supply Chain Management Professionals' annual State of Logistics reported that "US companies logged a record US $1.49T in shipping costs, up 6.2% year-over-year," which was US $250B more than what US companies spent on logistics in 2008.[117] Outbound shipping costs often "exceed all the costs of fulfillment added together—management, direct and indirect labor, packing materials, total occupancy, and allocated system

114 Stephan Serrano, "Top 10 Reasons (and Solutions) for Shopping Cart Abandonment," *Barilliance*, last modified August 5, 2020, https://www.barilliance.com/10-reasons-shopping-cart-abandonment/.

115 Courtney Reagan, "A $260 Billion 'Ticking Time Bomb': The Costly Business of Retail Returns," *CNBC*, December 16, 2016, https://www.cnbc.com/2016/12/16/a-260-billion-ticking-time-bomb-the-costly-business-of-retail-returns.html.

116 Ibid.

117 Nicholas Shields, "Shipping Costs Have Hit a Record High in the US," *Business Insider*, last modified June 22, 2018, https://www.businessinsider.com/us-shipping-costs-hit-record-high-2018-6.

costs."[118] Given these staggering numbers, along with shipping being one of the crucial factors driving business, it is especially surprising that shipping is one of the largest areas of static policies and egregious overspending.

RULES, TARIFFS, AND FEES, OH MY!

Shipment Pricing Hampers Business. In order to ship an object to a customer—either individual or business—the distributor must consider a dizzying array of factors. Once a package's real and dimensional weights are ascertained, the distributor must factor in the shipping service requirements of a multitude of carriers. Consider, for instance, all of the classes of mail offered by the USPS, as well as each class's rules, rates, and regulations.

Then there is the item's shipping location, in potentially several distribution centers, and possibly retail stores, relative to considering its eventual destination, as well as hundreds of different parcel and LTL carriers. There are, for example, regional carriers in different parts of the US: OnTrac in the West, Lone Star Overnight in the South, and Dicom in the Northeast/Canada, just to name a few.[119] Finally, carriers frequently change their rates and services. While these rates and services can be relied upon to change, the increment by which they do so is often unpredictable: "shipping rates will depend on the cost of fuel, how much people are using the mail class or lane,"[120] and so on.

118 "Do You Understand Where You're Losing Money on Shipping & Handling?" F. Curtis Barry & Company, accessed October 11, 2020, https://www.fcbco.com/blog/do-you-understand-where-youre-losing-money-on-shipping-handling.

119 Mark Scholz, "Regional Parcel Carriers—Why It's Wise to Expand Your Basket Beyond the Big 2," *Cerasis, a GlobalTranz Company*, accessed October 11, 2020, https://cerasis.com/regional-parcel-carriers/.

120 Desirae Odjick, "How Can I Reduce Shipping Costs as a Small Shop?" *Shopify*, last modified February 5, 2018, https://www.shopify.com/blog/competitive-shipping-as-a-small-shop.

So what do most businesses do? They err on the side of simplicity to keep things easy for the warehouse, and by doing so, they choose to spend more than they need to.

Order Fulfillment: Current State

According to LateShipment, "businesses that don't work with their carrier to map out shipping criteria can spend as much as 40 percent more in fees than those [that did]."[121] Remember, my sales team's research shows that shippers overpay for 22.3 percent of their shipments, or overpaid for slightly more than one out of every five shipments sent. This is calculated using only the shipper's current carrier makeup, before factoring in alternative shipping providers. The reasons for this are myriad, but can essentially be classified as the following: oversimplified carrier and service decisions, tariff complexity, human error, software, and packaging.

CARRIER PRICING PRACTICES—IT'S COMPLICATED

I want to warn you up front that carrier pricing practices are so complicated that it is difficult to talk about them. I'm going to do my best.

For starters, let's look at how many of these potential charges shippers are being subjected to in a parcel and LTL (less-than-truckload) environment. As you can see, the list goes on and on—fuel surcharges, residential delivery surcharges, delivery area surcharges, extended service area, oversize package surcharges, Saturday delivery, adult/direct/indirect surcharges, address correction, declared value, weekly service charges, origin/destination country surcharges, additional handling, additional handling non-stackable, dangerous goods (dry ice), dangerous goods (accessible), dangerous goods (inaccessible), delivery reattempt, COD, electronic COD, email return label, express tag, alternate address pickup fee, convenient delivery options, print return label, unauthorized package charge, inside delivery, inside

121 "Is Your Business Overspending on Shipping?" *LateShipment,* accessed October 11, 2020, https://www.lateshipment.com/blog/is-your-business-overspending-on-shipping/.

pickup, metro services area, missing or invalid account number, Northern Canada surcharge, payer rebilling, reroute of shipment.

I pulled this seemingly endless list from only *one* carrier's 2020 surcharge and fees updates page.[122] Not only that, but each of these fees vary by service and geographical region, making the permutations ludicrous.

Now imagine navigating these surcharges across multiple carriers, adding in the various services offered by each carrier in a warehouse setting where the operations worker is tasked with processing hundreds of orders per shift. Clearly, when there is no automation in place, i.e., a warehouse operator must know all the different carriers' rates, policies, services, etc. and be able to accurately and manually apply them to any given shipment, human error is significant. (Despite a pretty interface that may suggest otherwise, this is the reality. The major carriers forbid visual, side-by-side comparisons.[123]) Unless a shipping system is fully automated, with all decision-making trusted to rule-bound algorithms, mistakes will be frequent and costly. Static rule tables rarely resolve this. If we use an example of a warehouse fulfilling, say 2,000 shipments per day, operating at 99.5 percent accuracy, even that miniscule 0.5 percent error rate amounts to ten mistakes per day, or 2,500 per year in a 250-day work year, etc.

Item delivery is an intricate and complicated process, especially

---

122 "FedEx Shipping Rates," FedEx, last modified April 24, 2020, https://www.fedex.com/en-us/shipping/current-rates/surcharges-and-fees.html.

123 "User Guide: UPS Developer Kit," UPS, last modified 2017, http://www.ups.com/assets/resources/media/en_US/ups-dev-kit-user-guide.pdf.

Compare Two Shipping Carrier Options Side-By-Side Immediately," Shipping Easy, last modified December 15, 2016, https://support.shippingeasy.com/hc/en-us/community/posts/115000004083-Compare-two-shipping-carrier-options-side-by-side-immediately-.

when global destinations are considered. That's why it makes sense that pricing a diverse array of services would be difficult. Still, there seems to be no need for the minute aspect of carrier fee structures or the hidden nature of the charges.

Let's look at an example of an apparently adept operator who, despite his best efforts, is still subjected to considerable overpayment due to tariff complexity.

Consider the 2,000-parcel per month shipper. The company has undertaken what Trevor Outman of Shipware considers the two fundamental strategies in reducing shipping costs: operational improvements and carrier rate improvements.[124]

- **Operational improvements.** The company has invested in custom packaging to ensure that each parcel's DIM weight will never exceed its actual weight. It is zone skipping, which Outman, with some reservations, recommends as a useful fee-cutting maneuver: by consolidating or loading "hundreds of parcel packages into an LTL or TL freight shipment and line-hauling to a sorting hub that exists much closer to the end destination for all packages." Zone skipping allows shippers to "remove the higher cost of outer-zone (Zones 7 and 8, which is 1,401+ miles) shipments by replacing them with less expensive inner-zone (less than 600 miles, which is Zone 4; or less than 300 miles, which is Zone 3) shipments."[125] The shipper has invested in software that helps choose the least-cost service, as well as the proper service: "express shipments being delivered to Zones 2 or 3 (less than 300 miles) are being

124 Trevor Outman, "Reducing Parcel Costs: Operational Improvements vs. Carrier Rate Improvements," *PARCEL* (November–December 2017): 22-4. https://issuu.com/rbpublishing/docs/parcel_novdec_9ceb47df910285?e=2333928/55948760.

125 Ibid.

rerouted to ground delivery at a fraction of the cost with similar transit times."[126]

- **Carrier rate improvements (negotiations with carriers).** The company has negotiated a carrier contract with volume-based discounts, with a lower threshold of 1,500 parcels per month, and an upper of 2,500. Within these boundaries, the carrier offers the company a 42 percent discount on one- to five-pound ground deliveries, which suits its main shipping needs. Displaying some savvy, the company has also monitored their service usage and successfully requested a particular delivery area surcharge (DAS) mitigation, as it is an area to which 60 percent of their parcels are shipped. Lastly, they've negotiated an average yearly rate increase of 3.5 percent, far below the industry standard.

- **Result.** Despite all the work, this hypothetical company—which is doing more than most—is still extremely likely to be hit by all kinds of fees, surcharges, and rate changes. If, for example, they send 1,499 packages—or they barely miss their lower threshold—their agreed-upon shipping rates disappear, meaning that selling less merchandise can paradoxically end up costing the company more. Similarly, the always-there but often-hidden minimum charge heavily mitigates the percentage discount, such that actual savings are closer to 30 percent, and for some categories like Zone 2, one-pound shipments (the cheapest category in the company's boundaries), the real "discount" percentage can drop below 10 percent.[127]

---

126 Ibid.

127 Trevor Outman, "Minimize Shipping Costs with Parcel Data Analysis," *Supply & Demand Chain Executive*, last modified September 22, 2016, https://www.sdcexec.com/risk-compliance/article/12260763/minimize-shipping-costs-with-parcel-data-analysis.

ANALYZING PARCEL DATA

In 2017, "analyzing parcel data [was still] an exercise that most supply chain executives have yet to take advantage of," and "roughly 83 percent of organizations [weren't] utilizing big data analytics to improve their supply chain management" at all.[128]

Though the company was smart to take note of the surcharge—or accessorial—which previously cost them the most, they didn't take into account the almost endless list of other possible fees: "general rate increases (caps on the GRI), fuel surcharge (discounts on fuel), dimensional billing policies (Improved DIM factor and dimensional threshold), minimum charge (reduction per each service), rebates, early termination penalty, minimum commitment penalty, unfavorable thresholds on volume-based (earned discount tiers for FedEx and portfolio tiers for UPS), payment terms, and more," as well as "some of the common accessorial surcharges: residential surcharge discount, delivery area surcharge discounts (residential, commercial, resi & comm extended different for ground and express), additional handling fee discount, address correction discount, signature required discount, pickup fee discount, advancement fee discount, and many more."[129] With a partial list like that to keep track of, it's no surprise in a whack-a-mole way that "80 percent of all financial surcharge impact is derived from less than 20 percent of all the incurred accessorial categories."[130]

---

128 Ibid.

129 Trevor Outman, "Competing in the Online Retail World: Then and Now," *PARCEL*, last modified May 4, 2016, https://parcelindustry.com/article-4621-Competing-in-the-Online-Retail-World-Then-and-Now.html.

130 Trevor Outman, "Reducing Parcel Costs: Operational Improvements vs. Carrier Rate Improvements," *PARCEL* (November–December 2017): 22-4. https://issuu.com/rbpublishing/docs/parcel_novdec_9ceb47df910285?e=2333928/55948760.

Finally, the reduction of the average yearly rate increase unfortunately looks better on paper than in practice. The yearly rate increase is taken by averaging all of the rate increases in all of the different categories, such that, for example, FedEx's 2018 average rate increase was 4.9 percent, but its oversize charge increased by 10.34 percent, its residential surcharge by 7.79 percent, its delivery area surcharge by 8.33 percent,[131] and so on. Thus, though the negotiated rate of 3.5 percent is better than it could be, the company will feel increases beyond even the industry standard (of around 5 percent) through accessorial rates changing at very different paces.

I know, my brain hurts too.

DYNAMIC SOFTWARE SOLUTIONS

Due to these complexities, shippers are becoming increasingly reliant on dynamic software capabilities that are able to support real-time rates based on the parameters of carrier tariffs, company business rules, and comparative analytics. This is nowhere more evident than in the extraordinary example of the COVID-19 pandemic, in which there was a massive decline in global demand, but an equally massive uptick for a specific delivery service, last-mile/same-day, due to quarantining and social distancing. This, coupled with a diminished workforce, makes for higher carrier costs and slower delivery times, both of which—the costs and the times—shift rapidly.[132] Similar, yet less severe changes take

---

131 Trevor Outman, "6 Tips to Avoid Overpaying for Shipping," *Supply & Demand Chain Executive*, last modified October 10, 2017, https://www.sdcexec.com/sourcing-procurement/article/12373767/6-tips-to-avoid-overpaying-for-shipping.

132 "COVID-19: Briefing Note #3," McKinsey & Company, last modified March 16, 2020, https://www.mckinsey.com/business-functions/risk/our-insights/covid-19-implications-for-business.

place across the broader supply chain on a daily basis in the best of environments.

In situations far less extreme than a pandemic, however, carrier rates are rapidly and continuously changing. If a company can't depend on the real-time accuracy of its software, frequent, repetitive overpaying will happen. To compound this problem, in my experience, software business owners depend on effectively rate-shopping when, in reality, it accomplishes only an aggregation of carrier rates. Without specific order details on packaging, service level promises, and specific business rules that must be available at the point-of-sale and/or at the point of carrier selection, the shipping software itself is potentially a source of overpayment issues. It's a garbage-in, garbage-out problem. Either all the order data is accessible and contemplated in the rating process, or it's not. There is no middle ground, and no amount of customization or static rule manipulation can make up for the lack of complete and accurate data.

The accuracy of data inputs is just one aspect of the software automation need. All of this information is moot if the package itself has not been accurately accounted for. If, for instance, a shipping rate is quoted to a customer at the point of sale that does not factor in the final package's shipping weight and dimensions, the final cost is inevitably different and usually higher than the quote. This gap in automation—whereby a time-consuming portion of labor is given to weighing and measuring, rather than given to the system in a series of automated, rule-based if/then propositions—results in yet more chances for human error on top of the already inflated costs due to original misquotes and miscalculations.

My head of product loves to sum this up by asking prospects if they are running a multimillion-dollar business on $99 per month shipping software. The impending silence usually speaks for itself. Do the post-Christmas carrier invoices turn holiday cheer into post-holiday pink slips, like it did for that automotive parts distributor?

QUICK TAKEAWAYS

1. Your organization is almost certainly overpaying for shipping, but there is help. Consultants are available to help with tariff negotiations. Using an expert can be expensive, but they don't get paid unless you do. Take the opportunity and learn from it.
2. Due to carrier pricing tactics, it is likely you are not realizing the full discount you thought you had negotiated.
3. Carrier tariffs are too complex to properly utilize manually.
4. Entry-level and legacy shipping software products produce little more than carrier rate aggregation. They represent this as rate shopping, but real rate decisions require complete data, including specific order details on packaging (ship weight and dimensions), service level promises, and specific business rules. This information must be available wherever carrier rates are being determined.
5. Software must do the heavy lifting wherever possible to maximize rate utilization, carrier, and service selection.

CASE STUDY

For a real-life example of what it takes to set up a successful shipping operation, see the Skin Script and Verishop Case Studies in Appendix A.

CHAPTER 8

PACKING

Remember the movie *Tommy Boy*? "Fat guy in a little coat." For some reason, this song plays in my mind every time an Amazon or Target box shows up on my doorstep with a tiny object inside. "Fat box for a little thing..." I'll stop.

Before the major parcel carriers instituted dimensional pricing (a pricing policy based on package volume or, in other words, how much space a box occupies on a truck), many shippers didn't think much of packing efficiency. Today's shippers aren't just contemplating DIM weight charges, but also box-making hardware, smart-packing software, their environmental impact, and as e-commerce volumes continue to boom, the cost of the packaging itself. Let's dig in.

PACKAGING, ANOTHER OVER-EXPENDITURE

Packaging is another common area of over-expenditure in shipping. Most people have, at some point, received a shipment of a small object in a comparatively enormous package—again, Amazon is notorious for this. Though some have floated the theory that Amazon bases their packaging metrics on its various shipment cargo holds—a huge box for that tiny keychain makes all of a truck's boxes more steady relative to each other—the objections from fulfillment center workers that it's more to do with grabbing whatever packaging is handy in the limited time they have for each order seems more likely.[133]

In 2017, Amazon began approaching their infamous overpacking from many different angles: besides investing in on-demand machines that create "padded mailers...to fit smaller items" and poly bags instead of cardboard, Amazon also started working on algorithms to better assess what can be shipped together, and how. Finally, the giant also now ships items absent their "brick-and-mortar" packaging, which is designed to help products "stand out among a sea of choices," and tends to be "oversized with expensive and redundant shipping features," says Brant Nelson, senior manager of customer-packaging experience at Amazon. The Norelco OneBlade trimmer, for instance, is "sold in stores with 13 packaging pieces." For Amazon's customers, it produced a simple brown box, which is "about 80 percent smaller in volume than the box needed to ship the store version."[134]

This possible logic of packaging metrics is, however perversely, informed by DIM weight, or a package's dimensional weight, which considers, along with physical weight, the "space [a package] takes in the truck or plane." Carriers use DIM weight to maximize their own shipments, which comes in part through discouraging shippers "from including too much lightweight packaging materials or air in their parcels." If, however, companies are unaware of these

133 Augusta Statz, "Why Does Amazon Pack Small Items In Huge Boxes? This Question Plagues Its Customers," *Simplemost*, last modified June 25, 2018, https://www.simplemost.com/amazon-pack-small-items-big-boxes/.

134 Laura Stevens and Erica E.Phillips, "Amazon Puzzles Over the Perfect Fit—in Boxes," *The Wall Street Journal*, last modified December 20, 2017, https://www.wsj.com/articles/amazon-aims-for-one-box-fits-all-1513765800.

DIM weight policies or efficient packing strategies, experts estimate that "shippers who didn't adjust their packaging would see shipping cost increases of 5 to 25 percent."[135]

The highest volume shippers have historically negotiated sometimes significant accommodations on dimensional pricing—a key way they drive their distribution costs well below those of lower volume shippers. Whether it's by way of higher DIM factors, the calculation used to determine dimensional weight of a package, or getting certain dimensional fees waived entirely, the management of dimensional pricing is one more place where independents must be exceptionally good, because they don't have economies of scale to command the same concessions from the carriers.

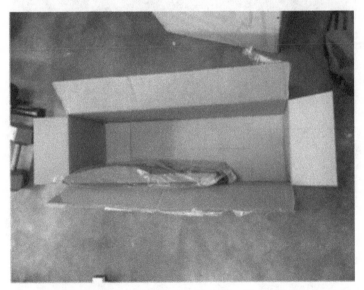

This picture is an AbMat (a pad used to isolate the upper and/or lower abs during an abdominal workout) purchased from a large fitness equipment retailer.

135 "Understanding FedEx® Dimensional Weight Pricing," *Shipware*, last modified April 5, 2019, https://shipware.com/blog/understanding-fedex-dimensional-weight-pricing/.

This picture is a stick of mascara purchased from a large CPG retailer.

This is a power strip ordered from an online retailer.

This is a picture of a golf scorecard ordered from a major marketplace.

This is a small box of earbuds.

This is a small box of earbuds from two angles.

FOUR PLASTIC HOCKEY STICKS

The worst offending shipment I've received was four plastic hockey sticks I purchased on Amazon for my boys' street hockey games. Each stick was forty-eight inches tall and twelve inches wide at the bottom, from heel to toe. The stick was less than an inch wide. All four sticks could have easily fit in a single box, but instead were shipped in four separate packages. Using FedEx's US ground DIM weight divisor of 139, I calculate 126# of additional dimensional weight. The excess packaging and space took up ten cubic feet on the truck, capacity that could have been used for other customer boxes.

SMART PACKING AKA *CARTONIZATION* AKA BIN PACKING AKA CUBING

Cartonization is the "algorithmic process which prepares orders for fulfillment by determining the quantity, size, and type of container required to optimize packaging."[136] Want the friendlier version? It's the technology used to answer the "which box" question.

Cartonization is a critical component of streamlined warehouse processes and provides a variety of benefits. One such benefit of cartonization is a reduction of damage during transit, which is one of the top reasons for merchandise returns. Citing a *Statista* estimate, Shopify analysts state that "in the US alone...return deliveries will cost $550 billion by 2020, 75.2% more than four years prior."[137] Research has shown that "replacing a damaged product can cost an e-commerce vendor up to seventeen times more than the original cost to ship."[138] Remember when I said there is leakage everywhere?

136 Raymond Cocozza, "How SKU Analysis Helps DCs Assess the Impact of SKU Proliferation on Their Operation," Conveyco, last modified June 9, 2020,https://www.conveyco.com/sku-analysis-sku-proliferation/.

137 Aaron Orendorff, "The Plague of E-commerce Return Rates and How to Maintain Profitability," Shopify, last modified February 27, 2019, https://www.shopify.com/enterprise/ecommerce-returns.

138 Kyla Fisher and Bob Lilianfeld, "Optimizing Packaging for an E-commerce World," Ameripen: American Institute for Packaging and the Environment, last modified January, 2017, https://cdn.ymaws.com/www.ameripen.org/resource/resmgr/PDFs/White-Paper-Optimizing-Packa.pdf.

Packing automation enables companies to hit the optimization sweet spot between potential damage, packaging costs, and packaging's impact on shipping costs. When linked with shipping software that can also algorithmically determine the best carrier for particular dimensional weight charges and delivery commitments, shippers are able to find not just the most cost-effective shipping method, but they also know this cost beforehand, allowing retailers to provide accurate shipping quotes at the point of sale and at the point of carrier and service selection.

BOXES ON DEMAND

If cartonization helps optimize packaging costs, it makes sense that a growing field within cartonization is that of "on-demand" packaging, or hardware that can make custom boxes on-site specifically for each order's unique makeup of items. Companies like Packsize advertise that on-demand packaging allows shippers to avoid the huge fees associated with DIM weights by minimizing "the amount of corrugated and filler material," cutting "box volume by an average of 40 percent, [helping] save valuable warehouse space, [reducing] environmental impact, and [eliminating] the risk of product damage due to box size."[139]

Packsize is a great solution for shippers of all sizes, not just because of the direct benefits of its hardware, but also because they have moved the large, up front costs normally associated with complex hardware and robotics to a variable cost model.

Amazon, of course, has implemented on-demand boxing in its fulfillment centers, reporting "that its centers are able to keep working and producing boxes all day long, without having any

---

139 "Dimensional Weight Calculator," Packsize: On Demand Packaging, accessed October 11, 2020, https://www.packsize.com/dim-weight-charges/.

downtime because the boxes are produced while the products are coming out from their warehouse. The operator no longer has to go looking around the warehouse to find the right box for the product."[140]

Proper cartonization software, like ShipHawk, when used in conjunction with box-making machines, also reduces the labor required to prepare and pack orders. Smart-packing algorithms rely on sophisticated systems of record. For cartonization purposes, these algorithms must reference inventory data concerning the "size, weight, height, width, length, and category"[141] of objects. The software can then calculate the ideal box size based on the item weight, dimensions, and other characteristics (value, fragility or special handling requirements) and communicate this data directly to the box maker instead of relying on a human at a pack station and their trusty, but costly, tape measure and manual input.

THE NICHE MARKET OF CUSTOM PACKAGING

Along with cartonization, packaging issues have led to the niche market of custom packaging, which is primarily for shippers with predictably sized shipments. Custom packaging can meet precise packing guidelines for the correct dimensions, as well as produce greater brand control over the entire business-to-consumer experience, down to the unboxing. Custom packaging is regularly used by subscription box companies like Blue Apron and Birchbox, but it's also found in retailers who are sensitive to design and every

---

140 "Box on Demand Improves Amazon Shipping Time, Costs, Quality," Tappi, accessed October 11, 2020, http://www.naylornetwork.com/ppi-otw/articles/index-v2.asp?aid=332978&issueID=42762.

141 Josh Bond, "Cubing and Weighing: Besting the Dim Rate Dilemma," *Modern Materials Handling*, last modified November 1, 2015, https://www.mmh.com/article/cubing_and_weighing_besting_the_dim_rate_dilemma.

element of the customer experience like Apple and their famous iPhone packaging, and skincare company, Glossier.

As the dad of three boys, I'd be remiss if I didn't point out one amazing example of custom packaging creativity in the Nike Adventure Club, a subscription that comes with new kids' shoes, fun activities, and a box that is begging for markers and crayons to color it. Whoever designed this product, I love you and think you deserve an award.

However, whether through cartonization or customization, cardboard and its durability, lightness, and cheapness have all been challenged by new synthetic materials. Perhaps most ubiquitously, many companies have begun shipping lightweight, non-fragile objects in polyethylene mailers, which are water-, tear-, and puncture-resistant. For objects requiring slightly more protection, there are padded poly mailers, which hardly weigh more than their counterparts.[142]

APPLE'S PAPER AND PACKAGING STRATEGY

Most American homes have numerous Apple devices laying around. From iPhones and iPads to MacBooks, monitors, cables, and headphones, Apple's fame isn't only a result of their products, but their attention to every element of the customer experience, right down to their custom packaging. Apple's product packaging has received enough attention to warrant publishing a white paper on it, which is referenced

---

142 "4 Ways You're Overspending on Shipping," *Shippingeasy*, last modified June 1, 2018, https://shippingeasy.com/blog/4-ways-youre-overspending-on-shipping/.

below. In it, they detail their commitment to the environment, efficiency, sourcing, and long-term packaging strategy.[143]

PACKAGING AND THE ENVIRONMENTAL IMPACT

For both business and environmental reasons, however, the answer to packaging problems cannot come from more fossil-fuel products. While consumers want cheap, fast shipping options, they also expect "easy disposal of packaging materials," with a quarter of those surveyed expressing annoyance with "packaging material that was difficult to recycle or unrecyclable." In addition, over 78 percent of consumers voiced that a company's e-commerce packaging is "reflective of its environmental values."[144] The consumer's desire for recyclability and the company's desire for packaging efficiency can often be at odds, but they don't necessarily have to be. As Ben Conwell, retail expert, notes, "When it comes to packaging, what's good for business is good for the Earth."[145] As 33 percent of our landfills are filled with packaging materials, cutting back on overpackaging helps companies' bottom lines as much as it does the environment. According to Hanko Kiessner, CEO of Packsize, "the average box is 40 percent too large for its contents...If excess volume were reduced, it would eliminate 24 million of the 60 million truckloads of product shipped annually in the United States," which would, in turn, "save 1.75 billion gallons

143 "Apple's Paper and Packaging Strategy," Apple, last modified October 2017, https://www.apple.com/environment/pdf/Packaging_and_Forestry_September_2017.pdf.

144 Kyla Fisher and Bob Lilianfeld, "Optimizing Packaging for an E-commerce World," Ameripen: American Institute for Packaging and the Environment, last modified January, 2017, https://cdn.ymaws.com/www.ameripen.org/resource/resmgr/PDFs/White-Paper-Optimizing-Packa.pdf.

145 Benjamin Conwell, "Successful and Sustainable Shipping—It's All About the Box," *Cushman & Wakefield*, last modified February 11, 2019, https://www.cushmanwakefield.com/en/united-states/insights/us-articles/2019-02-indust-successful-and-sustainable-shipping.

of diesel, preventing 17 billion kilograms of carbon dioxide from entering the atmosphere."[146]

We also must consider the impending disaster in the recycling industry. Plastic, as we're coming to learn, isn't really recyclable at all. Its once-appealing durability also makes it an "environmental time bomb. An estimated 90.5 percent of all the plastic produced since 1950 is still in existence," and "only 8.4 percent of plastic waste in the US was recycled in 2017."[147] Since 1950, "the world has created 6.3 trillion kilograms of plastic waste—and 91 percent has never been recycled even once."[148] "When it comes to plastic," a recent *Rolling Stone* article states, "recycling is a misnomer." As Jim Puckett, executive director of the Basel Action Network, said, "they [Big Plastic; a corporate supergroup of Big Oil and Big Soda with a puff of Big Tobacco, responsible for trillions of plastic cigarette butts in the environment every year] really sold people on the idea that plastics can be recycled because there's a fraction of them that are. It's fraudulent. When you drill down into plastics recycling, you realize it's a myth."[149]

With China now refusing essentially all plastic products for recycling—"saying that its own recycling industry was becoming an environmental hazard"[150]—finding sustainable, efficient methods of packing and shipping should be high on the priority list.

---

146 Gary Forger, "Sustainable Packaging Is Ready to Make ts Mark," *Logistics Management.* Online, last modified September 1, 2019, https://www.logisticsmgmt.com/article/ sustainable_packaging_is_ready_to_make_its_mark.

147 Vivienne Walt, "Plastic that Travels 8,000 Miles: the Global Crisis in Recycling," *Fortune*, last modified March 16, 2020, https://fortune.com/longform/plastics-global-recycling-problem/.

148 Tim Dickinson, "Planet Plastic," *Rolling Stone*, last modified March 3, 2020, https://www. rollingstone.com/culture/culture-features/plastic-problem-recycling-myth-big-oil-950957/.

149 Ibid.

150 Ibid.

Many companies are now effectively using sustainable materials inside their shipping cartons. Paper packing, air pillows, and biodegradable packing peanuts that "decompose in water, leaving no toxic waste"[151] are becoming more prevalent.

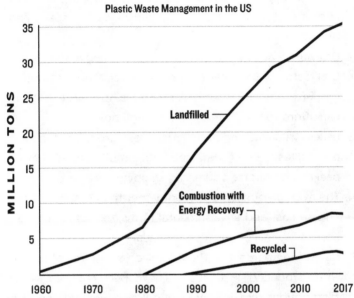

Plastic Waste Management in the US

"Plastics: Material-Specific Data," US Environmental Protection Agency (EPA), accessed October 11, 2020, https://www.epa.gov/facts-and-figures-about-materials-waste-and-recycling/plastics-material-specific-data.

151 "Biodegradable Peanuts," *ULINE*, accessed October 11, 2020, https://www.uline.com/ BL_2001/Biodegradable-Peanuts?pricode=WE442&Sitelink=US_Google_Cushioning-Foam_Group_41_Peanuts_Biodegradable-Peanuts&gclid=EAIaIQobChMIxKGGzI2l6QI Vex-tBh0J5AW6EAAYASABEgJoQPD_BwE&gclsrc=aw.ds.

QUICK TAKEAWAYS

1. Don't rely on manual box selection efforts at your pack stations. Investigate cartonization software like ShipHawk, box-making machines like Packsize, consulting services and/or custom packaging to minimize wasted space and dollars.

2. Be aware that your competitors may have negotiated better DIM factors, which may materially reduce their distribution costs for similarly sized orders—this is how large retailers can afford to send small items in large boxes.

3. Excessive packaging designed to make products stand out on shelves is being replaced with simple, cost-effective packaging built for optimizing shipping cost.

4. The average box is 40 percent larger than it needs to be. This, in cost and environmental terms, results in an additional sixty million truckloads annually.

5. Ninety-one percent of the 6.3 trillion kilograms of plastic waste produced since 1950 has never been recycled. Recycling options remain limited, and buyers are taking notice and demanding better material choices. Do your part. The packing materials you use matter. Limit the use of nonbiodegradable plastic whenever possible.

CASE STUDY

Read about how one startup handled pick and pack complexity as their business rapidly scaled in The Black Tux Case Study in Appendix A.

CHAPTER 9

WAREHOUSING

In ShipHawk's early days, I opened a warehouse for a customer who was growing fast and needed help. So, we did what we do best. I think back to this time fondly, not because we opened a new DC in rapid fashion and helped the customer catch up on a backlog of orders, a job that was well outside our core focus, but because I took my wife and boys with me on the adventure. The warehouse was dirty, which boys love, and huge, which boys also love. They played while we worked. Then I caught one of my sons chewing on a pallet. It only took one lip splinter for the fun to end. I'm sure you can imagine the breakdown that ensued.

My sales team frequently thinks of warehouses as fitting into one of two categories: "owned" warehouses or 3PL (third-party logistics) warehouses. The primary motivation is to determine who has control over the levers that can help or hinder an operator— levers like throughput, order routing, and carrier relationships. It's hard to help shippers who don't have control over their product distribution. This sounds bad, but it's not, I promise. As we will see, there are many reasons for utilizing 3PLs, and third-party operations come in many different flavors.

As we proceed, it's important to consider your current business stage and growth rate. These two factors, more than many others, will help you determine the path that's right for your warehouse strategy.

WAREHOUSE UTILIZATION

Warehouses are expensive, and they keep getting more expensive every year. In an annual survey conducted by Warehousing & Fulfillment, data shows that between 2017 and 2018, warehouse space went up just more than $1.25 per square foot (per year), from $6.53 in 2017 to $7.79 in 2018.[152] The growth of e-commerce has led to a rapid rise in demand for industrial real estate. Indeed, in July 2020, CNBC reported that the "demand for industrial real estate could reach an additional 1 billion square feet by 2025 [...]."[153] This is in addition to industrial real estate's "absorption of nearly 1.4 billion square feet" from 2014 to 2018.[154] Growing inventories, which are now frequently in the millions and have also grown in diversity and complexity, further compound the problem, increasing the amount of space many sellers need to store their goods. So prevalent are these growing e-commerce inventories that the very concept long ago (2004) acquired its own name: the "Long Tail" of online retailers, with something for everyone, no matter how niche.[155] Along with increased facility costs from additional

---

152 "Warehousing and Fulfillment Fees According to Latest insightQuote Survey," *Warehousing and Fulfillment*, last modified February 26, 2019, https://www.warehousingandfulfillment.com/warehousingandfulfillment-news/warehousing-and-fulfillment-fees-rise-according-to-latest-insightquote-survey/.

153 Lauren Thomas, "U.S. May Need Another 1 Billion Square Feet of Warehouse Space by 2025 as e-Commerce Booms," *CNBC*, last modified July 9, 2020, https://www.cnbc.com/2020/07/09/us-may-need-another-1-billion-square-feet-of-warehouse-space-by-2025.html.

154 Saurabh Mahajan, "The Future of the Industrial Real Estate Market," *Deloitte*, last modified May 30, 2019, https://www2.deloitte.com/us/en/insights/industry/financial-services/future-of-industrial-real-estate-market.html.

155 Chris Anderson, "The Long Tail," *Wired*, last modified October 1, 2004, https://www.wired.com/2004/10/tail/.

space, SKU proliferation can also lead to "increased order cycle time, decreased accuracy, and trapped capital."[156]

In addition to spending time focusing on driving down shipping costs, operators must also focus on properly managing their real estate and the working capital challenges that accompany this capital-intensive area of the business.

Many approaches have been used to drive down these hard costs. One frequently celebrated example is the just-in-time (JIT) management of inventory. By receiving inventory just before it is needed, sellers have historically been able to reduce or, in some cases, even eliminate safety stock, the additional inventory held on shelves meant to reduce the risk of running out. Many sellers using this lean manufacturing approach ground to a halt as the COVID pandemic made its way around the globe. I heard many newscasters saying, "You can't ship the car if it's missing one part."

WHAT IS LEAN MANUFACTURING?

Lean manufacturing, or lean production, is a production method derived from Toyota's 1930 operating model, "The Toyota Way" (Toyota Production System, TPS). The term "lean" was defined as "...a way to do more and more with less and less—less human effort, less equipment, less time, and less space—while coming closer and closer to providing customers exactly what they want.[157]

---

156 Cocozza, Raymond, "How SKU Analysis Helps DCs Assess the Impact of SKU Proliferation on Their Operation." June 9, 2020. Conveyco. Online,https://www.conveyco.com/sku-analysis-sku-proliferation/.

157 "Lean Manufacturing," *Wikipedia*, accessed May 24, 2020, https://en.wikipedia.org/wiki/Lean_manufacturing.

Even before the pandemic, businesses struggled with balancing inventory supply with customer demand. One of the most public examples was the Whole Foods implementation of its then-new inventory management system, order-to-shelf (OTS). The system was implemented to reduce "unnecessary" inventory (remember, the inventory is only unnecessary if there aren't customers ready to buy it), to reduce costs and spoilage, and to reduce labor costs. As Whole Foods shelves lay bare and employees were left dealing with angry customers, workers began describing OTS as "militaristic" and "morale-crushing." "Entire aisles are empty," one employee was quoted as saying.[158]

Many customers blamed Whole Foods' parent company, Amazon, but the truth is, for many businesses, inventory is a difficult problem to solve. Whether you are the one who decides to hold safety stock or the one who orders everything just-in-time, it can be an expensive problem.

These and the myriad of other costs that go into running a DC are why utilization is key. I'm not just talking about floor space. I'm talking about the entire cube.

I've toured countless warehouses where the management team insists that they are "out of space" and "need to find another location." I look up and see enough air space to kitesurf from one side of the building to the other. In other operations, I've seen floor to ceiling racks, sometimes double stacked, well-used mezzanine levels, and thoughtful design clearly bent on utilizing every square inch of the building, wall to wall, and floor to ceiling. New ware-

---

158 Hayley Peterson, "'Entire Aisles Are Empty': Whole Foods Employees
    Reveal Why Stores Are Facing a Crisis of Food Shortages," *Business
    Insider*, last modified January 18, 2018, https://www.businessinsider.com/
    whole-foods-employees-reveal-why-stores-are-facing-a-crisis-of-food-shortages-2018-1.

house construction has made full cube utilization even easier. In the 1960s, the average warehouse height was twenty-four feet. By 2016, it had climbed to thirty-three feet.[159]

From a hard cost and working capital perspective, it's a rookie move to expand to multiple warehouses without first fully leveraging one strategically located DC. An optimal scenario would be to distribute from one warehouse, either company-owned or via a 3PL partner, where you can fulfill across any channel you choose. This setup requires the lowest working capital commitment.

Of course, this scenario is stage-based. If your business is big, you may need multiple facilities in multiple locations. When you do expand, there are several options to consider, from opening a new company-owned facility, to a dynamic warehouse where you can rent as little as a single pallet space, to partnering with a 3PL, to a cross-docking approach, which I believe will continue to grow in popularity. So how do you determine which is the best choice for your business? Let's explore each option in detail.

MULTI-WAREHOUSE AND DYNAMIC/POP-UP WAREHOUSE STRATEGIES

If 90 percent of all Americans living within fifteen miles of a Walmart is the company's biggest asset in retaining its top retailer spot and key to its future of a two-hour delivery strategy, it makes sense for other distributors to follow suit, at least minimally. Amazon, of course, "with DCs in almost every state, can deliver to 44 percent or more of the US population in four hours

---

159 Jeff Berman, "As e-Commerce Grows, so Does the Height of Warehouses, Says CBRE," *Logistics Management*, last modified March 28, 2017, https://www.logisticsmgmt.com/article/as_e_commerce_grows_so_does_the_height_of_warehouses_says_cbre.

or less."[160] As speed and cost of shipping increasingly become two of most companies' biggest obstacles, many have invested in multiple distribution centers, either by building their own satellite locations or by outsourcing to 3PLs across the country. Costs aside, there are many benefits to operating out of more than one location: multiple inventory locations mitigate risk factors including weather, in-house catastrophes, such as electrical fires and the like, and natural disasters. They also produce faster delivery times and lower shipping costs as each order can be "routed to and shipped from the closest fulfillment center [to the customer],"[161] both of which can lead to a competitive advantage.[162]

Research shows that with one strategically placed DC, companies can reach 73 percent of the US via ground shipping in two days. With two DCs, this number jumps to 90 percent, to 91 percent with three, and to 95 percent with four distribution points.[163] That strategic placement, however, is everything: 60 percent of the US population resides within 600 miles of Ohio,[164] and more than half within 650 miles of Nashville, Tennessee.[165] In addition to population access, companies must consider a host of other

---

160 Brian Barry, "How to Assess if Multiple Distribution Centers Can Reduce Shipping Costs and Time to Consumer," *F. Curtis Barry & Company*, accessed October 11, 2020, https://www.fcbco.com/blog/bid/360921/multiple-dcs-may-be-best-way-to-reduce-shipping-costs-and-transit-times.

161 Kristina Lopienski, "What is Distributed Inventory? 3 Benefits of Using Multiple Fulfillment Centers (& How to Do It)," *ShipBob*, last modified January 31, 2020, https://www.shipbob.com/blog/3-benefits-using-more-than-one-warehouse-e-commerce-fulfillment/.

162 "Benefits of Having Multiple Distribution Centers," *Swiss Mail Solutions*, last modified April 4, 2018, https://www.swissmailsolutions.com/benefits-of-having-multiple-distribution-centers/.

163 "COVID-19: Shipping & Fulfillment Continuity Action Plan," ShipHawk, last modified March 2020, https://info.shiphawk.com/covid-19-shipping-and-fulfillment-continuity-action-plan-social.

164 Tom Feran, "Gov. John Kasich Says 60 Percent of U.S. Population Is within 600 Miles of Ohio," *PolitiFact*, last modified May 13, 2011, https://www.politifact.com/factchecks/2011/may/13/john-kasich/gov-john-kasich-says-60-percent-us-population-with/.

165 "U.S. Population Around Nashville," Nashville Area Chamber of Commerce, accessed October 11, 2020, https://s3.amazonaws.com/nashvillechamber.com/Maps-ECD/NationRadius1.pdf.

factors in moving to multiple-warehouse shipping: the location must take into account the availability of "affordable, high-quality labor, proximity to key roadway and other transportation systems, cost of business, a business-friendly environment, and options of expanding."[166]

In addition to multiple warehouses, many companies are exploring the relatively new possibilities of dynamic and pop-up warehouses. Dynamic warehouse strategies offer "infinitely flexible" warehouse networks in part by enabling businesses to reconsider what exactly a warehouse is.[167]

Some dynamic warehouse options operate out of empty space in existing 3PL operations while others use old shopping malls, retail stores, or other real estate strategically located close to dense consumer populations. Think of the Halloween superstore that pops up every year. Using the same logic, dynamic warehouse networks allow companies to store merchandise in temporary locations that they don't own. As 70 percent of companies queried reported that they don't have "a viable solution" when experiencing "significant fluctuations in volume at specific times throughout the year,"[168] dynamic warehousing and pop-up warehouses are innovative solutions.

Not only do dynamic warehouses offer temporary storage and fulfillment services, they also frequently support cross-docking,

166 Karen Thuermer, "Warehouse & Distribution Center Site Selection: Seeking a Skilled Workforce." *LogisticsManagement*, last modified August 4, 2017, https://www.logisticsmgmt.com/article/warehouse_and_distribution_center_site_selection_seeking_a_skilled_workforce.

167 Morgan Hass, "The New Logistics Part 2: Dynamic Warehouse Networks," *Flexe*, last modified February 8, 2016, https://www.flexe.com/blog/the-new-logistics-part-2-dynamic-warehouse-networks.

168 Karl Siebrecht, "The New Logistics Part 1: Pop-Up Warehousing." *Flexe*, last modified February 3, 2016, https://www.flexe.com/blog/the-new-logistics-part-1-pop-up-warehousing/.

where bulk orders can be received, sorted, and reshipped to the end customer without the need for overnight storage. I have seen these services speed delivery times, reduce product handling, and at times, bypass the need for storage completely. Large carriers and 3PLs have used cross-docks for years to speed service and reduce storage costs. Dynamic warehousing options are now making these services accessible to smaller shippers. Think of it like a nationwide directory of distribution points you can instantly tap into.

I'm not going to spend too much time on inventory management tactics. At the very least, I suggest all shippers use a WMS (warehouse management system) of some type. Larger companies have entire teams dedicated to inventory management, but small and midsize shippers don't have that luxury and frequently struggle with inventory costs and positioning. One simple strategy for managing inventory across multiple distribution points is to separate your inventory into three categories—the fast-moving SKUs, the slow-moving SKUs, and those in the middle. Keep your fastest moving products in the most locations, the middle group in only a couple of locations, and the slow movers in only one DC. This strategy will allow you to get your fast-moving items to customers quickly, and you won't have to purchase an excess of slow-moving items just to keep them in stock in each location.

FULFILLMENT BY AMAZON

It's easy to see the appeal of a program like Fulfillment by Amazon (FBA)—sellers gain access to Amazon's enormous customer base, and as David Heacock, CEO of FilterBuy said, "[g]etting started is certainly easier than setting up your own website and warehousing infrastructure. Create your product listing, send inventory to an

FBA warehouse, and you are in business."[169] While its advantages may be clear, FBA's drawbacks are considerable and surprising. While it can "offer unmatched potential for sales," Amazon's huge cut of every transaction ensures that "the house always wins."[170]

That huge cut isn't necessarily straightforward. Similar to the complexity of carrier tariffs, there are listing fees, subscription fees, return administration fees, storage fees, long-term storage fees, closing fees, high-volume listing fees, and so on.[171] In addition, these fees—especially the storage fees, a key component of FBA—can quickly function more like penalties. "If you have products sitting too long at an Amazon warehouse then you are going to pay through the nose for them."[172] In addition, these fees are ever-increasing and differ during peak times. In 2020, for example, sellers with "items [that] fall in the medium oversize category...will see a whopping increase of around 14.7 percent."[173] The majority of sellers on the "Is there anyone who makes money using FBA?" forum hosted by *Amazon Services* report 15 to 20 percent profit margins.[174]

Finally, there is Amazon's seller policy, which is so complex that

169 Pamela N. Danziger, "Thinking of Selling on Amazon Marketplace? Here Are The Pros and Cons," *Forbes*, last modified April 27, 2018, https://www.forbes.com/sites/pamdanziger/2018/04/27/pros-and-cons-of-amazon-marketplace-for-small-and-midsize-businesses/#7a40cdcd6867.

170 Ibid.

171 Dave Hamrick, "Amazon FBA Fees, How They Work, and How to Profit as a Seller," *JungleScout*, last modified February 7, 2020, https://www.junglescout.com/blog/amazon-fba-fees/.

172 Gerard Adlum, "What Life Is Really Like As an Amazon FBA Seller," *eDesk*, accessed October 11, 2020, https://blog.edesk.com/resources/life-as-an-fba-seller/.

173 Dave Bryant, "Amazon FBA Fees in 2020 Are Going Up a LOT," *Ecomcrew*, accessed October 11, 2020, https://www.ecomcrew.com/amazon-fba-fee-increases-for-2020/.

174 "Is There Anyone Who Makes Money Using FBA?" Amazon Services Seller Forums, accessed October 11, 2020, https://sellercentral.amazon.com/forums/t/is-there-anyone-who-makes-money-using-fba/437777.

there is "a growing industry of consultants who help sellers navigate the ruthless world of Marketplace and the byzantine rules by which Amazon governs it."[175] As truly nightmarish scenarios are not uncommon (consider, for example, Kevin Harmon, whose entire business of used DVDs—169,013 units sold in a year and a half—was terminated overnight by Amazon after a counterfeit complaint. After losing all of his merchandise to Amazon and being successfully sued by the manufacturer, Harmon finally saw a photo of the counterfeit object in question and realized that the DVD wasn't even his. Amazon had incorrectly fulfilled an order under his seller number using its "co-mingling" strategy.[176]), sellers increasingly need all the protection they can get.

3PLS

Third-party logistics (3PL) are third-party businesses whose services are various elements of warehousing and fulfillment. Third-party logistics are so diverse these days that the term is rather meaningless when used alone as a tool for sourcing a warehousing or fulfillment partner. Many 3PLs represent a vast array of services marketed to businesses of any size, but the *everything-for-everyone* approach is not only unhelpful, it is frequently misleading. All 3PLs weren't created equal.

When a business owner or executive goes looking for a 3PL partner, they are usually looking to solve specific problems or augment their current operations with specific levers. Some are looking for storage solutions or low-friction access to new distribution

175 Josh Dzieza, "Prime and Punishment: Dirty Dealing in the $175 Billion Amazon Marketplace," *The Verge*, last modified December 19, 2018, https://www.theverge.com/2018/12/19/18140799/amazon-marketplace-scams-seller-court-appeal-reinstatement.

176 Kevin Harmon, "Third Party Sellers Need To Rethink The Amazon FBA Program," *StartupNation*, last modified May 22, 2013, https://startupnation.com/start-your-business/plan-your-business/amazon-fba-program/.

points. Others want to take advantage of 3PLs' advanced technology to improve pick, pack, ship efficiencies, and processing times, as many 3PLs have invested in advanced robotics and software solutions that smaller companies can't afford. Some want to outsource the entire returns process. Still, others just want the discounted shipping rates that they can't access through carriers directly. (Carriers hate this, by the way!) Even those looking to outsource everything behind the buy button need a 3PL suitable for their size, stage, and inventory makeup. There are 3PLs for businesses of every size and stage, and there are 3PLs built to handle nearly all inventory types: oversized, refrigerated, those requiring assembly, subscription box, and HAZMAT (hazardous materials). In addition, most 3PLs will fulfill orders across any channel and can include marketplace services like Seller Fulfilled Prime (SFP), as long as order processing SLAs (service level agreements) are adhered to. A 3PL can be a great alternative for Amazon Marketplace sellers who don't want to use FBA.

Where many companies go wrong with 3PL relationships is that they fail to manage their 3PL partner like they manage their own operation. They don't track metrics, set targets, and manage their teams and their 3PL partners to those goals. This includes order processing times, damage, mispicks (returns), and shipping costs.

When we sign a new customer at ShipHawk, I sometimes order their products. I try to order the same product through each channel they utilize in an effort to understand how their customer is experiencing the relationship and to identify opportunities for improvement. Buyers always know where frustrations lie.

Let me share a recent example. We signed a customer who sells on Amazon and through their own website. Amazon fulfills the Vendor Central shipments, and the company's 3PL partner fulfills direct orders. I ordered the same item from Amazon and from the company's website. The Amazon order status was updated regularly, and the delivery showed up in two days. The 3PL order took one week, and I received no status updates.

As a buyer, the difference was material and it was not a result of the 3PL's capabilities. It was the result of a lack of service standards enforced across both channels. The Amazon order was significantly less profitable for our customer, but by way of the delivery experience, the company was incentivizing me to return to the channel producing the worst margin. This problem could have been avoided through the proper use of data.

Lesson: only you can decide whether an owned or 3PL facility is right for your business and your stage. Whichever way you go, make sure you manage them to the same standards. And don't let your kids chew on pallets. Spouses don't easily forget mistakes like that.

QUICK TAKEAWAYS

1. Warehouse location makes a difference. Ninety percent of the US is reachable via ground shipping in two days with two properly positioned DCs.
2. It may make sense for your business to consider an additional company-owned warehouse or shipping option from a 3PL partner to drive down shipping costs and/or meet delivery expectations.
3. Working with a marketplace 3PL like Fulfillment by Amazon (FBA) may provide customers with faster service, but with scale, at a materially higher cost.
4. Dynamic warehousing companies like Stord, Flexe, or Flow-

Space offer easy-to-scale, low-commitment storage, and fulfillment services that may help augment company-owned warehouses.

5. Cross-docking may help improve delivery times while reducing storage costs.
6. Manage your 3PL like it's your own warehouse.

CASE STUDY

Different products frequently necessitate different warehouse strategies. See a real-life example of warehouse strategy come to life in the Floyd Home Case Study in Appendix A.

CHAPTER 10

DATA AND ANALYTICS

Peter Drucker, author of *The Effective Executive* (as well as thirty-eight other books) and who has been described as "the father of modern management," said, "If you can't measure it, you can't improve it."

I am routinely shocked by the thousands of business owners and company executives my sales team connects with who do not have defined supply chain goals aside from "more," "faster," or "cheaper," and who don't maintain accurate data so as to measure progress or success. My hope is that if you take only one thing from this book, it's this: set fulfillment and shipping goals and set up the infrastructure to measure progress toward those goals, holding your team accountable for the successes and failures. This move alone will put you ahead of 90 percent of the independents in the market.

That being said, the reality of today's competitive threats requires more than just setting and measuring goals. That is only step one. Luckily, there are modern tools that can help facilitate more advanced uses of data.

KEY METRICS AND AUTOMATED DECISION-MAKING—A LOVE STORY

As we've discussed, various market demands—such as rapid order processing and seasonal fluctuations—are forcing DCs to become more flexible so they can better react to market changes and become more proactive in the future. On the one hand, the traditional "linear and sequential" approach of supply chain management no longer suits the terrain, as "globalization, resource scarcity, and cost reduction [extend] supply chains, creating multilayered ecosystems that encompass distant and sometimes volatile geographies."[177] On the other hand, many larger, more established companies are still firmly entrenched in dated systems, relying on single-sourcing with one major carrier, static logic for service decision-making, and packing decisions that are either complex and custom, but still static, or overly simple and reliant upon complementary carrier rate negotiations, which rarely match the need completely. As DCs fulfilling orders for a handful of known and predictable items become increasingly rare, the methods of dealing with new business realities must change in accordance. If pop-up warehousing is a "hardware" solution to one such issue reflective of new market demands and realities, the use of data and analytics is a far larger software strategy.

In a 2020 consumer products industry outlook, Deloitte declared that those companies who wished to compete in the future climate of Industry 4.0 must commit themselves now to "investing in digital technologies with built-in analytic capabilities" that can lead to the development of "data analytics and intelligent decision-making capabilities," as well as the "leveraging [of] consumer insights to guide investment decisions." But, as the outlook was

---

177 "Why Exception Management Is Taking Center Stage for Supply Chain Visibility," *OpenText*, last modified October 24, 2018, https://blogs.opentext.com/why-exception-management-is-taking-center-stage-for-supply-chain-visibility/.

also quick to point out: "collecting data is just the first step. Data is only useful to the extent that it can be harnessed to generate insight."[178] Data and analytics, as we'll see in more depth, is such a useful tool for companies, not just because it can provide answers to crucial questions, but also because it forces companies to figure out which questions are most pressing for their business.

WHAT IS INDUSTRY 4.0?

Industry 4.0 is the "trend towards automation and data exchange in manufacturing technologies and processes which include cyber-physical systems (CPS), the internet of things (IoT), industrial internet of things (IIOT), cloud computing, cognitive computing, and artificial intelligence."[179]

BIG DATA AND WAREHOUSE AUTOMATION

Most warehouses generate a ton of data every hour of every day, whether it's recorded or not. This can include employee data—such as wages, salaries, headcount, etc.—inventory and order data—such as quantity, location, open orders, net demand, etc.—fill rates, on-time performance, cancellations, returns, on-hold orders, waitlist orders, promise dates, and so on. When you begin to introduce external data points—shifting carrier rates, the weather, etc.—not to mention other internal data streams such as warehouse hardware functionality and the like, the term "Big Data"—meaning a final data set whose complexity is beyond not only simple human calculation, but older forms of data analysis—makes sense.

---

178 "2020 Consumer Products Industry Outlook," Deloitte, *accessed October 11*, 2020, https://www2.
     deloitte.com/us/en/pages/consumer-business/articles/consumer-products-industry-outlook.html.

179 "Industry 4.0," Wikipedia, accessed April 30, 2020, https://en.wikipedia.org/wiki/Industry_4.0.

The purpose of Big Data is not just to consume and organize large quantities of data, but to reveal trends, patterns, and hidden associations between datasets. Historically, this task has been so large that a customer once shared with me his personal efforts to mitigate the obstacles. Prior to implementing a more modern ERP in NetSuite, which was directly connected to ShipHawk's TMS, he had a team of five data people who did nothing but "clean up" the data that was spit out of his legacy software. This from a forward-thinking operator who obviously takes data very seriously and was looking for better visibility into his business long before software solutions supported his needs.

Like we've seen with automation more broadly, Big Data is a field with many subsets. Those with the most impact on warehouse automation currently are:

1. The use of data for predictive analytics or "intelligent decision-making capabilities"
2. Smart/connected warehouses
3. Exception monitoring and management, aka "visibility"

PREDICTIVE ANALYTICS—SEEING THE WAREHOUSING FUTURE

Data, especially something as vast as Big Data, is useful only in so far as it can be put to work—all of the data at Google's behest, for example, is useless to most users without the ability to easily search it via query. For example, if a company decides to focus on a particular KPI, such as shipping time, a data and analytics approach would begin by collecting historical and current information concerning this KPI, sometimes from informational areas not typically associated with a given indicator. For shipping time, data such as "item information for each SKU handled, order history information for past year and peak season, forecast [of] demand details, order details, location in warehouse, inbound receipt data, [and] customer data"[180] just to name a few, would be collected. Such internal datasets and samples allow companies to evaluate different, disparate metrics relative to each other. Is there, for instance, a relationship between certain zip codes or lanes and longer shipping times that the aggregate data hides?

Once relevant external datasets and samples are introduced, such as shipment cost trends, and competitors' relative shipping practices, companies can begin to "visualize trends and areas for opportunity [by] turning large quantities of data into accessible insights."[181] (Learn more about shipping data and analytics at jeremybodenhamer.com/shipping-data.) This can be achieved through "customized scheduled reporting," including the use of data for predictive models of future company behavior and growth, including "seasonal fluctuations and demand for warehouse expansion."[182]

There are many software products on the market to facilitate the collection and interpretation of Big Data. Shippers can choose between supply chain specific solutions from companies like ShipHawk, Blue Yonder, or IBM Supply Chain, and more general business intelligence solutions like Looker, Sisense, Tableau, or Domo.

---

180 Richard Koch, "The Three Phases of Distribution Center Optimization," *Chainalytics*, last modified June 16, 2015, https://www.chainalytics.com/distribution-center-dc-optimization2/.

181 "Real-Time Shipping Data & Analytics," ShipHawk, accessed October 11, 2020, https://shiphawk.com/shipping-data/.

182 Ibid.

SMART WAREHOUSES

I know for a fact that Siri is the source of 90 percent of my boys' jokes, even though they swear otherwise. I've heard "What does a raincloud wear under its coat?" a thousand times. ("Thunderwear" in case you are wondering.) They have clearly mastered the finer benefits of the modern virtual assistant. Chatbots like Siri are being baked into all sorts of "things," and in the process, using famed venture capitalist Marc Andreessen's words, eating the world. One by one, as companies connect devices to the internet, and in many cases, integrate a voice assistant, they are turning once mundane devices into exciting, intelligent, hungry monsters. From smart speakers and thermostats to doorbells and sprinklers, these devices never stop creating data and can be connected to any number of other devices, powering them to perform feats that were previously unimaginable. Have you seen a network of smart light bulbs?

A similar movement has been happening in warehouses around the globe. Once-dumb warehouses have come alive and can now be made into never-ending gobstoppers of data. One of data's greatest uses is in the building, operating and maintaining the warehouse itself. A smart warehouse can be thought of as the culmination of automation, in which every operation has been reconsidered through the lens of data, robotics, the Internet of Things (IoT), and AI. In addition, these operations are integrated with one another, often by means of their software or hardware automations. As discussed throughout this book, these operations include "identifying and receiving orders, counting products, storing products, and remembering where they are later and sending orders to the correct place."[183] Smart warehouses "approach their operations as a series of interconnected operations, processes, and resources,

183 Margaret Rouse, "Smart Warehouse," *IoT Agenda*. Online, accessed October 11, 2020, https://internetofthingsagenda.techtarget.com/definition/smart-warehouse.

each deserving attention and critical examination to promote efficiency, with the goal of lowering time and cost to perform."[184]

Frequently used in smart warehouses, IoT is "the interconnection via the internet of computing devices embedded in everyday objects, enabling them to send and receive data." IoT offerings are beginning to be explored in earnest by various DCs and shippers because not only do warehouses generate tremendous amounts of data concerning what might be called the "visible" aspects of business mentioned above, they also generate data concerning "invisible" aspects, such as HVAC system readings, building humidity, hardware usage, etc.—all of which can be monitored through "sensors and intelligent management systems," which, when linked to "IoT applications and cloud-based devices are expected to ease building management," as well as to "ensure greater efficiency and better performance of the entire facility."[185]

Smart warehouses take the warehouse and its performance into account, and not just as a space to be optimally filled and used. As Dave Hopping, president of Siemens Smart Infrastructure Solutions & Services America's, says, "many buildings already generate volumes of data through cameras, thermostats, alarms, and monitors, but much of it is not being used in an integrated fashion."[186] As with other instances of data and analytics usage, smart warehouses can analyze seemingly disparate datasets to show their interdependence, thereby "better [predicting] long-term maintenance and operational performance over the life

---

184 "What is a Smart Warehouse? Third Party Logistics," *Nebraska Warehouse*, accessed October 11, 2020, https://nebraskawarehouse.com/smart-warehouse-third-party-logistics/.

185 Craig Guillot, "The Path to Smart Distribution Centers Begins with Data," *Supply Chain Dive*, last modified April 17, 2018, https://www.supplychaindive.com/news/smart-distribution-centers-data-JDA-Deloitte/521542/.

186 Ibid.

of the building." With warehouses built from the ground up as smart, "sensors could even be used to track individual movements throughout a building to analyze processes and workflows relative to building design. This data could then be used for the design of future distribution centers or to optimize existing ones."[187]

This back-and-forth between spatial design and actual everyday use has a long history, particularly in town and urban planning. There are the sanctioned lines of travel—such as sidewalks, promenades, boulevards—and so-called "desire lines," or the routes people actually take. Here, at least, data and analytics are upgrading an old practice employed previously, albeit less technologically. When a university campus in Buffalo, New York, was redesigned, for example, the architect left the new grounds entirely pathless and covered in uniform gravel. When snow blanketed the area in the winter, he went up in a helicopter and took aerial photographs of the paths people were forging of their own accord through the campus space. He then remade these paths on the ground, following the same widths according to usage that had been tracked out in the snow.[188] Smart warehouses are doing the same or similar things, with the use of sensors and iterative building design.

Not only would smart technology help manage buildings through communicating "predictive maintenance" for things like "conveyor belts, rider trucks, and racking, but also building systems such as HVAC and security," its largest impact would be felt in data and analytics' predictive abilities, "before humans can see it." Machine learning, as it is called, could "reduce downtime and increase efficiencies in many ways," such that buildings "would be able to continually run analysis to predict equipment failures

187 Ibid.

188 Ryan Gander, *Loose Associations and Other Lectures* (Paris: onestar press, 2007), 19–20.

before they happen or anticipate security needs based on trends and predicted movements of occupants. As buildings become smarter, they'll eventually become autonomous and 'always learning,'" says Hopping.[189]

A great example of this is replicating the ingenious low-tech layout process used in Buffalo but in the digital environment. It's called a digital twin which is "a digital replica of potential and actual physical assets (physical twin), processes, people, places, systems, and devices..." Warehouse data from all sources, the "internet of things, artificial intelligence, machine learning, and software analytics" is then integrated with spatial network graphs of physical elements in an effort to determine optimal warehouse layout. In addition, once set up, the digital twin "continuously learns and updates itself from multiple sources to represent its near real-time status, working condition, or position." Digital twins can also be fed historical data for additional comparisons.[190]

VISIBILITY

The amount of internal data most companies generate is staggering, so it may be daunting to also consider factoring in external data! These increasingly large datasets are precisely those of Big Data. By using platforms such as IBM Blockchain, companies are able to better interact with their own and others' data. The need for such services, such as IBM Blockchain's Rapid Supplier Connect, which quickly connects buyers and suppliers, has been especially crucial during the COVID-19 pandemic. Had the state of California better utilized such systems, they might not have

---

189 Craig Guillot, "Robots as a Service: A low-risk path to warehouse automation?" *Supply Chain Drive*, last modified September 3, 2019, https://www.supplychaindive.com/news/robots-as-a-service-a-low-risk-path-to-warehouse-automation/562136/.

190 "Digital Twin," Wikipedia, accessed June 1, 2020, https://en.wikipedia.org/wiki/Digital_twin.

spent over $1 billion on a deal with BYD, an iffy supplier of masks, for which the federal government denied safety certification.[191]

In more general circumstances, using such tools forces companies to consider possible impacts and repercussions where they might not have previously, as well as to put themselves into a more proactive, rather than reactive, position. In the context of warehouse automation, nontraditional data are all those sources that might be able to help companies better predict market volatility and demand unpredictability. As the supply chain and thus DCs become increasingly globalized, these sources must also account for "an increasing number of disastrous events that potentially disrupt or completely stop the supply chain."[192] Nontraditional data can include the macro—like social media trends, foreign affairs, geopolitics, and natural phenomena—as well as the micro—like "outdoor temperature, educational test scores for the school district the supplier is located in, number of doctors within 50 miles, number of other businesses open and closing within 50 miles of a supplier,"[193] and the list goes on. All of these hopefully put companies in a better position from which to understand and assess "true root causes" of the events that manifest within the warehouse as various volatilities or demand spikes/slumps often before they happen.

As can be seen, all these particular aspects of data and analytics share a predictive function. This is not due to any kind of digital

191 Dustin Gardiner, "Trouble for Gavin Newsom's $1 Billion Mask Deal: Feds Reject Safety Certification," *San Francisco Chronicle*, last modified May 13, 2020, https://www.sfchronicle.com/politics/article/Trouble-for-Gavin-Newsom-s-1-billion-mask-15268320.ph.

192 "Why Exception Management Is Taking Center Stage for Supply Chain Visibility," *OpenText*, last modified October 24, 2018, https://blogs.opentext.com/why-exception-management-is-taking-center-stage-for-supply-chain-visibility/.

193 William Scott Hunter, "Real-Time Supply Chain Predictive Metrics," (PhDdiss., Missouri University of Science and Technology, 2012), 53.

mysticism or magic, but simply a vast increase on both sides of an "if/then" function: as companies can allow for millions of possible *ifs*, their ability to either design or allow for machine learning to design an equal amount of *thens* naturally puts organizations in a better position from which to mitigate risk and calamity. Thus, the idea of "exception management" is truly an issue of data management, which allows companies to make visible and actionable previously unknown and unquantifiable externalities.

The COVID-19 pandemic is an ultimate example of globalization in many different forms, and its effects on the supply chain have been especially catastrophic. Though there are undoubtedly many exception management lessons to be learned here, it might be best to consider a far simpler instance, one with which we are all familiar.

Shipping time. The KPI mentioned above is a known indicator for most DCs and shippers. Exception management, however, can also uncover new possible KPIs or underthought of areas in which performance is less than optimal, and for which analytic solutions can help. An application like Waze aggregates data from its users in order to help drivers avoid traffic by alerting them ahead of time, as well as offering alternative routes. Imagine this with far more data input sources, as well as with more end goals than simply arriving at a destination. If, for instance, a truck will be thirty minutes later than expected at a warehouse, this fact might be known ahead of time, the information is then relayed, and "all warehouse operations can respond based upon that change" rather than simply delaying all operations by that same thirty minutes. In this way, "dwell time"—accounting for a possible "$40bn a year in lost productivity among warehouse operations, truck drivers and logistics providers"[194]—is dramatically reduced, causing a ripple effect of increased productivity across the organization.

QUICK TAKEAWAYS

1. Most companies do not have specific shipping and fulfillment goals and metrics. Establishing these goals should be priority #1.
2. Many larger companies are still reliant on legacy systems and static logic for advanced and complex decision-making.
3. Data can be immensely valuable, but only if it is collected and put to work. Big Data is too big to treat as a single project. Specific goals related to areas of focus like warehousing, hardware, people, or orders must be established prior to putting data systems in place.
4. Big Data may lead executives to consider solutions beyond one's immediate operation. A good example of this is carrier/shipment exception management.
5. There are software products available to help with each of these like:
   - Supply chain specific solutions from companies like Ship-Hawk, Blue Yonder, or IBM Supply Chain provide data access and visualization.
   - General business intelligence (BI) solutions like Looker, Sisense, Tableau, or Domo provide data and visualization across the entire business.
   - Exception Management solutions like Convey focus on exception management related to parcel and home deliv-

194 "Welcome to the World of Data-Driven Analytics," *SupplyChainBrain*, last modified May 24, 2019, https://www.supplychainbrain.com/articles/29742-welcome-to-the-world-of-data-driven-analytics.

eries, while companies like Narvar focus on shipping notifications and returns. There are many more than I have listed here.

CASE STUDY

See how a fast-growing startup is using data to compete head-to-head with Amazon in the Grove Collaborative Case Study in Appendix A.

CHAPTER 11

ROBOTS AND ROBOTICS

My boys break things, and frequently each other, so robots are not high on our gift list. The closest we've gotten to toy robots in our house are the numerous drones I've brought home from trade shows. (Yes, I am the dad who goes booth-to-booth asking for three pieces of schwag because I can't bring home just one.) The roof of the elementary school near our house is now home to all of those drones. Every. Single. One.

THE ROBOTS OF YESTERDAY

Much like toy robots, out of all the sectors of automation, robots and robotics tend to get the most attention, and it's not hard to see why. With their sci-fi appeal for both good and evil, robots are an easy symbol of technology's pros and cons. The good vs. bad robot argument reminds me of the Pixar movie, *WALL-E*. WALL-E (Waste Allocation Load Lifter: Earth Class) is a trash compactor robot who falls in love with EVE (Extraterrestrial Vegetation Evaluator). He follows her across the galaxy and battles against his evil robot nemesis, AUTOPILOT, all in the name of robot love. There is lots of G-rated robot fighting if you are a parent of kids who love robot battles.

Though always linked to the future—although usually not as sweetly as in *WALL-E*—robotics has been around for some time. The first robot—capable of moving material about a dozen feet or so—was patented in 1954 by George Devol, and General Motors installed its first robot (weighing 4,000 pounds and costing $25,000 or $237,238 today[195]) in a New Jersey plant in 1961.

Used with permission from the Robotic Industries Association and the Association for Advancing Automation (merging in 2021), https://www.robotics.org/joseph-engelberger/unimate.cfm.

Unsafe to be used around humans, early robots were suitable only for industrial manufacturing and "initially focused on shifting dangerous or harmful jobs to robotic technology."[196] Fast-forward some fifty years, and some aspects of robotics can be found in most sectors, from warehouses and fulfillment centers to a variety of industries.[197] Many warehouses are adopting some form of robotics technology with more expected. The 2017 estimates figured the

195 Rebecca J. Rosen, "Unimate: The Story of George Devol and the First Robotic Arm," *The Atlantic*, last modified August 16, 2011, https://www.theatlantic.com/technology/archive/2011/08/unimate-the-story-of-george-devol-and-the-first-robotic-arm/243716/.

196 Ruthie Bowles, "Warehouse Robotics: Everything You Need to Know in 2019," *Logiwa*, last modified August 24, 2020, https://www.logiwa.com/blog/warehouse-robotics.

197 Will Allen, "Guide to Warehouse Robots: Types of Warehouse Robots, Uses, Navigation & More," *6 River Systems*, last modified August 28, 2020, https://6river.com/guide-to-warehouse-robots/.

and used for smaller, repetitive tasks such as picking facilitation and in-warehouse transport.

WAREHOUSE ROBOTICS MARKET

"Warehouse robots in the "0.5 kg to 10 kg (1.10 lbs to 22 lbs) range held the largest share of the warehouse robotics market in 2016."[205]

Though picking and in-warehouse transport might be two of the biggest uses for robots, they have been shown to improve productivity throughout operations. AGVs like "automated forklifts" help warehouses speed up tasks like loading and unloading, and when equipped with grippers, palletizing, and depalletizing. Robotic arms embedded with cameras are able to sort items by looking at an object and comparing it with other similar images via internal software: "robotic sorting solutions reduce the number of touches, transfers, and conveyors needed compared to traditional sorting systems."[206] As warehouses grow taller, "climbing" AS/RS, such as the Skypod, are becoming more common.[207]

At the distribution centers of MSC Industrial Supply—a large distributor of metalworking, maintenance, and MRO products and services—the company stands ready to ship over 1.5 million products at any given time. To assist in their largely B2B operations, the company partnered with Plus One Robotics. Speaking of this collaboration, Doug Jones, MSC's chief supply chain officer, said, "We've been able to stand up a robot that is serving as a packing

---

205 Ibid.

206 Ibid.

207 Bowles, "Warehouse Robotics."

operator [and] currently packing about 600 orders per day."[208] Using Plus One's proprietary hardware/software combination, MSC's robotic pack station includes an arm equipped with perception or vision capabilities. This perception then allows the robot to pack accordingly, given what it knows about whatever product with which it's currently dealing.

Given the huge number of possible products, as well as their frequently changing packaging and other factors of visual change, the robot does not—nor is it expected to—always know what it's packing. "If that robot gets stuck trying to do a task," continued Jones, "we actually have a human that we call our crew chief that is back in San Antonio, Texas at our Plus One Robotics headquarters who sees what the robot sees through its vision and will tell the robot how to pick up an item." Each time something like this happens, the robot is also learning: "as we get more and more trials in front of that robot, that robot becomes smarter and smarter," said Jones.[209]

This system, in which many robots have one human overseer or crew chief, is part of what Plus One Robotics' CEO and co-founder Erik Nieves calls "the missing middle" in robotics—halfway between total autonomy like those robotic arms on automotive assembly lines and zero autonomy, as with surgical robots directly manipulated by one surgeon.[210] According to Nieves, "What's missing, and where the real action is, is the missing middle of supervised autonomy: one person responsible for many

---

208 Plus One Robotics, "MSC Automated Packing Application," YouTube, last modified March 3, 2020, https://www.youtube.com/watch?v=OQC9tf01ZL8&feature=emb_logo.

209 Ibid.

210 Plus One Robotics, "The Missing Middle—Supervised Autonomy for Robots," YouTube, last modified September 10, 2019, https://www.youtube.com/watch?v=-jfojf7OUhQ&feature=emb_logo.

robots…"[211] As Jones said, "We're not putting robots in to replace all of our great associates at our distribution centers. We see applications in our distribution centers where there's just not a lot of value-add that the human brings—repetitive tasks, maybe things that are ergonomically not fun. We're looking to put robots in those types of places so we can take our valuable human associates and put them in more value-add type positions."[212]

ROBOTICS-AS-A-SERVICE

As with many other types of hardware-based automation, the introduction of robotics can seem cost-prohibitive. New industrial robotics can cost between $50,000 and $80,000, and up to $150,000 once "application-specific peripherals are added."[213] In many cases, these costs don't include software integrations and the technical consultants needed to build out internal systems workflows. "Traditional system integration (making one system "talk" to another) has been responsible for more project glitches and postponements than any other form of technical hurdle."[214]

This isn't to say costs haven't come down as more players have entered the market. There are less expensive robots, but even those systems come with high system integration fees and can easily outpace the cost of the hardware.

Although custom robotics installations have projected not-instant ROIs like shipping software, a properly configured system can

211 Ibid.

212 "MSC Automated Packing Application."

213 "How Much Do Industrial Robots Cost?" *RobotWorx*, accessed October 11, 2020, https://www.robots.com/faq/how-much-do-industrial-robots-cost.

214 Jason Kingdon, "Robotic Automation: Another Moore's Law?" *Wired*, accessed October 11, 2020, https://www.wired.com/insights/2014/04/robotic-automation-another-moores-law/.

BIG DATA, AI, AND MACHINE LEARNING

"Data is only useful to the extent that it can be harnessed to generate insight."[219] So, how, exactly, do we generate insight? For the most part, this is done through software that can help provide companies with better visibility, be it improved KPIs, predictive algorithms, or exception monitoring. Another, perhaps more abstract way in which Big Data can both generate insight and then be put to work is through robotics. Robots using Big Data's insights can happen in two ways.

First, consider a company for whom an internal data analysis revealed an abnormally long pick time in one area of the warehouse. Further inspection showed a design error in that area that effectively doubled pick times. Robots, however, would

219 "2020 Consumer Products Industry Outlook," Deloitte, *accessed October 11*, 2020, https://www2.deloitte.com/us/en/pages/consumer-business/articles/consumer-products-industry-outlook.h

prove that there is bleeding everywhere. "Even if a robot and a person take up the same number of square feet at the point of work, the robot still has a smaller 'enterprise footprint.' Robots don't need entry halls, break rooms, parking spaces, bathrooms, etc. They take up less room when viewed from the overall facility perspective. Imagine the amount of space you would free up if half your staff was suddenly glued to the floor," Nieves points out. Not only can robotics reduce labor, turnover, warehouse space utilization, and downtime costs, savings can be found in areas that are not as apparent. Proving Nieves's point, I have a friend who did a major installation, reducing his labor requirements in one facility by 80 percent. What he didn't anticipate was that his parking needs would also drop by 80 percent, allowing him to renegotiate his lease and significantly reduce his overall real estate cost.

The up-front cost of robots may price out many shippers who don't have large amounts of capital available. And for good reason. Designing, building, and selling robots is expensive. I was once approached by a couple of Google engineers who were also aspiring startup entrepreneurs who saw a potential opportunity for less expensive, easier-to-access fulfillment robots. I told them then and it remains the case that there is a huge, unmet need due to high hardware and integration costs. Our best hope is that Moore's Law will apply as successfully to robotics as it has in other areas, giving smaller companies access sooner, rather than later.[215]

For now, Robotics-as-a-Service (RaaS) is aiming to meet at least part of the need by lowering the financial entry point. RaaS providers offer the rental of any number of robots due to specific warehouse needs, be they task-, season-, or space-dependent. As Melonee Wise, CEO of Fetch Robotics, said, "These scalable deliv-

others? According to Plus One Robotics' CEO and co-founder Erik Nieves, the answer is an emphatic no. "This is a bifurcated market," he says, in which there are six big players and "the next 94 is pretty much everybody else." The next ninety-four "behave differently, buy differently, have access in some ways to fewer resources. It's a different game." Acknowledging that robotics is one possible means of these "next ninety-four" keeping pace and defending themselves, Nieves points out that "even if there's six or seven big users in the Americas, there's only five systems integrators of any scale." None of those five providers are equipped to handle the needs of midsize or smaller retailers, as "they're overwhelmed

216 Craig Guillot, "Robots as a Service: A low-risk path to warehouse automation?" *Supply Chain Drive*, last modified September 3, 2019, https://www.supplychaindive.com/news/robots-as-a-service-a-low-risk-path-to-warehouse-automation/562136/.

217 "50,000 Warehouses to Use Robots by 2025 as Barriers to Entry Fall and AI Innovation Accelerates," *ABI Research*, last modified March 26, 2019, https://www.abiresearch.com/press/50000-warehouses-use-robots-2025-barriers-entry-fall-and-ai-innovation-accelerates/.

218 Ibid.

215 Ibid.

ROBOTS VS. HUMANS

The delicate balance between automation and the promises of productivity and efficiency it offers on the one hand, and the role of human labor on the other, is nowhere more evident than in the field of robotics. Feeding into preexistent sci-fi clichés, the idea of "robot overlords" seems closest to fruition in fulfillment centers. Amazon's FCs have attempted to ease the transition into robotic management while at the same time asking its workers to behave more robotically. In one such instance, called gamification, workers race "to fill customer orders, their progress reflected on a screen in their workstation in video game format. Their physical actions, assembling orders, and moving items, are translated into virtual in-game moves. So, the faster someone picks items and places them in a box, for example, the faster their car will move around a virtual track."[227]

The games simultaneously register the completion of "...(a) task, which is tracked by scanning devices, and can pit individuals, teams, or entire floors against one another to be fastest."[228] I guess you could say it's kind of like the movie *Tron* when Flynn enters the digital realm. Only he's not a freedom fighter for the oppressed programs of the grid (aka warehouse workers). He's only entrusted with a tape gun and protective goggles instead of a neon motorcycle and light sword. Excited yet? If he posts a poor score, he's not exploded into a cloud of pixels. No, he's fired. If he does place high enough, he gets a ten-dollar T-shirt or a two-dollar water bottle.[229]

[227] James Vincent, "Amazon Turns Warehouse Tasks into Video Games to Make Work 'Fun,'" *The Verge*, last modified May 22, 2019, https://www.theverge.com/2019/5/22/18635272/amazon-warehouse-working-conditions-gamification-video-games.

[228] Ethan Baron, "Amazon Pits Warehouse Workers Against Each Other, Eyes Robot Replacements with Steel Talons," *The Mercury News*, last modified May 22, 2019, https://www.mercurynews.com/2019/05/21/amazon-pits-warehouse-workers-against-each-other-eyes-robot-replacements-with-steel-talons/.

[229] Vincent, "Amazon Turns Warehouse Tasks into Video Games to Make Work 'Fun.'"

Horror stories abound.[230] In fact, one previous Amazon warehouse worker wrote an entire book on her experience.[231] Though it's one of countless such tales, consider Amazon's CamperForce. Designed as one response to labor shortages, CamperForce workers are "around traditional retirement age, in their sixties or even seventies," who are "glad to have a job, even if it [involves] walking as many as 15 miles a day on the concrete floor of a warehouse."[232] Many of these "workampers," as they're called, have "seen their retirement savings vanish in the stock market or lost homes to foreclosure." As one of CamperForce's recruiters said, "We've had folks in their eighties who do a phenomenal job for us...You guys have put in a lifetime of work. You understand what work is."[233]

MY MANAGER IS A ROBOT

As Josh Dzieza said in a recent *Verge* article, "[W]hile we've been watching the horizon for the self-driving trucks, perpetually five years away, the robots arrived in the form of the supervisor, the foreman, the middle manager."[234] Manager robots are found in many different sectors, in two different capacities. In the first, the robot holds a worker's tasks, assignments, and goals. In the second, the robot monitors that worker's labor: "[W]hen rate-tracking programs are tied to warehouse scanners or taxi drivers

---

230 Shannon Liao, "Amazon Warehouse Workers Skip Bathroom Breaks to Keep Their Jobs, Says Report," *The Verge*, last modified April 16, 2018, https://www.theverge.com/2018/4/16/17243026/amazon-warehouse-jobs-worker-conditions-bathroom-breaks.

231 Heike Geissler, *Seasonal Associate* (South Pasadena, CA: Semiotext(e), 2018).

232 Jessica Bruder, "Meet the CamperForce, Amazon's Nomadic Retiree Army," *Wired*, last modified September 14, 2017, https://www.wired.com/story/meet-camperforce-amazons-nomadic-retiree-army/.

233 Ibid.

234 Josh Dzieza, "How Hard Will The Robots Make Us Work?" *The Verge*, last modified February 27, 2020, https://www.theverge.com/2020/2/27/21155254/automation-robots-unemployment-jobs-vs-human-google-amazon.

are equipped with GPS apps, it enables management at a scale and level of detail that [Fred, father of Taylorism] Taylor could have only dreamed of. It would have been prohibitively expensive to employ enough managers to time each worker's every move to a fraction of a second or ride along in every truck, but now it takes maybe one."[235]

Under this level of scrutiny, workers have found themselves trying to meet increasingly unrealistic productivity quotas in what was an already demanding environment. Jonathan Meador, an employee at an Amazon FC in Tracy, California, equipped with Roomba-shaped robots, watched as "pickers and packers were expected to move more products every minute, and more boxes shot down the conveyor belt."

"Before robots," he said, "it was still tough, but it was manageable... Afterward, we were in a fight that we just can't win."[236] (Oh, but you can win, Jonathan. You can win T-shirts!) Indeed, workers at FCs and DCs with robotics have far higher injury rates than those without—at that same Amazon FC in Tracy, for instance, the "serious-injury rate there nearly quadrupled, going from 2.9 per 100 workers in 2015 to 11.3 in 2018."[237]

This is the opposite of what robots were supposed to do! Even in their worst scenarios, in which they stole jobs and automated industries so fully as to replace the human worker completely, the robot was not supposed to make the working conditions of human laborers more dangerous or exploitative. Robotic automation was

---

235 Ibid.

236 Will Evans, "Ruthless Quotas at Amazon Are Maiming Employees," *The Atlantic*, last modified December 5, 2019, https://www.theatlantic.com/technology/archive/2019/11/amazon-warehouse-reports-show-worker-injuries/602530/.

237 Ibid.

intended to "eliminate some of the most menial warehouse labor," and to remove the worker from dangerous, repetitive, often stultifying work. Robots were to be the ones "walking" over ten miles a day on concrete warehouse floors. And today they do. "I doubt any associate at Amazon or a 3PL using Locus or 6River would choose to go back to the old way of walking the aisles all night," said Nieves.

These efficiencies should then allow companies to upskill their workers by helping "employees develop new technical skills to move into better-paying jobs."[238] (Like I wish I could develop the skills I need to keep my boys' drones off their school roof!) Examining how and why this hasn't happened means also examining the role of the worker more broadly in the context of automation.

238 Jason Del Rey, "How Robots Are Transforming Amazon Warehouse Jobs—For Better and Worse," *Vox*, last modified December 11, 2019, https://www.vox.com/recode/2019/12/11/20982652/robots-amazon-warehouse-jobs-automation.

QUICK TAKEAWAYS

1. Robotics will have a significant impact on productivity, but they aren't right for every shipper, and they are expensive. If you can access robotics and the integration services needed to get them operable and maintained, make sure the ROI is better than the alternatives. Robots-as-a-Service (RaaS) is a step toward making robotics more accessible to smaller shippers.

2. Robots can be used hand in hand with machine learning (ML) to make continual, automated adaptations to real-life circumstances.

3. The relationship between robots and humans in the warehouse is fragile. Yes, most warehouse robots are taking over where the people were already more or less acting as robots. Relieving them of the monotony and strain is the humane thing to do. Don't forget, many of these jobs are not pleasant. The people in the warehouse should not be treated like machines. Doing so hurts workers and the business.

4. Robots should be used to replace people where they can automate work that is difficult, dangerous, or expensive for humans to do, thereby creating opportunities to invest in upskilling workers for jobs where they can add more value.

CASE STUDY

For a real-life example of robots and robotics in action, see the Tipsy Elves Case Study in Appendix A.

CHAPTER 12

OPERATIONS WORKERS

#HEROCLASS

On May 6, 2020, nine US senators wrote a letter to Amazon CEO Jeff Bezos, asking why the company repeatedly terminated "workers who raise health and safety concerns."[239] The COVID-19 pandemic ratcheted up the attention on warehouse worker safety, and Amazon had fired at least four workers who had made the public aware of the ongoing threats to employee well-being within the company.

Maren Costa was one of the terminated employees. She "was a member of Amazon Employees for Climate Justice, and had been publicly supporting warehouse workers' advocacy, including offering to match donations 'to support [her] Amazon warehouse colleagues and their communities, while they struggle to get consistent, sufficient protections and procedures from [Amazon].'[240]

---

239 "Letter to Amazon from Senators Warren, Sanders, Booker, Brown, Colleagues," *United States Senate*, last modified May 6, 2020, https://www.warren.senate.gov/imo/media/doc/2020.05.06%20 Letter%20to%20Amazon%20from%20Senators%20Warren,%20Sanders,%20Booker,%20 Brown,%20colleagues.pdf.

240 Maren Costa(@marencosta), "I Am Matching Donations [...]," Twitter, last modified March 27, 2020, https://twitter.com/marencosta/status/1243585580736237568.

Another, Emily Cunningham, "was also a member of Amazon Employees for Climate Justice" and "had circulated a petition calling on Amazon to 'expand sick leave, hazard pay, and child care for warehouse workers,' and 'temporarily shut down facilities where workers were confirmed to have the virus so the facilities could be sterilized.'"[241]

As the working class of the world suffered by way of job losses or the inability to shelter in place because they were essential and too poor to stop working, industry giants saw profits soar.

A coalition of workers from Amazon, Whole Foods, Target, Walmart, and FedEx staged an unprecedented walkout to protest employee health and safety during the pandemic. "These workers have been exploited so shamelessly for so long by these companies while performing incredibly important but largely invisible labor," said Stephen Brier, a labor historian and professor at the CUNY School of Labor and Urban Studies.[242]

The pandemic has brought these workers and the critical, but low-paying work they perform out of the shadows and into the light. "All of a sudden, they're deemed essential workers in a pandemic..."[243]

The never-ending push for productivity, whether in an effort to meet skyrocketing demand during a global pandemic or to squeeze in more orders per shift by way of intermixing operations workers

---

241 Bridget Read, "The Women Who Criticized Amazon—and Got Fired," *The Cut*, last modified April 24, 2020, https://www.thecut.com/2020/04/amazon-tech-workers-fired-coronavirus.html.

242 Daniel A. Medina, "As Amazon, Walmart, and Others Profit Amid Coronavirus Crisis, Their Essential Workers Plan Unprecedented Strike," *The Intercept*, last modified April 28, 2020, https://theintercept.com/2020/04/28/coronavirus-may-1-strike-sickout-amazon-target-whole-foods/.

243 Ibid.

and robotic counterparts, has made the treatment and conception of labor and its role in the supply chain an ongoing and escalating concern. We frequently connect labor, and indeed many of the issues of automation we've spoken of thus far to ideas of progress, productivity, and efficiency.[244] Yet, at times, we fail to ask: to what end?

As ideas of efficiency have become so deep-rooted in our business advancement efforts, the relative quality of supply chain jobs and warehouse operation jobs, in particular, has plummeted. This is partially due to global anti-unionization efforts. Consider, for example, the International Longshore and Warehouse Union, which is especially active on the West Coast of the US. About half of their members make more than $100,000, with some foremen and managers making over $200,000—all of whom get free healthcare.[245] Part of this union's staying ability and salary control has come from sharing "in the gains from innovations in efficiency, such as modern shipping containers" as well as from worker solidarity. In the 1930s, all West Coast ports were organized under a single contract, thereby preventing "shipping companies from pitting workers at neighboring ports against one another."[246]

Across the Pacific, however, port workers at Hong Kong's Kwai Tsing Terminals—which in 2013 controlled as much as 70 percent of the cargo flowing through the Hong Kong port—faced wildly

244 Though it might be a bit of an oversimplification, economists use "productivity" in the same way that the business sector uses "efficiency," and so the two are used here simultaneously.

245 Chris Kirkham and Andrew Khouri, "How Longshoremen Command $100k Salaries in Era of Globalization and Automation," *Los Angeles Times*, last modified March 1, 2015, https://www.latimes.com/business/la-fi-dockworker-pay-20150301-story.html.

246 Ibid.

different conditions and wages, and nonexistent benefits.[247] In 2013, workers there organized a strike to protest all of the above, including wages that had not only stagnated but gone down in relation to inflation. Mr. Lee, a dock worker who had "barely seen a rise in his income in the last 10 years," said, "I've been working in this industry for 20 years. There's been two adjustments both in wage reduction and increment, but the rate was very low. Basically, there's no fringe benefits; we only had paid leave in recent years. My monthly income isn't steady.[248]...Of course, it's difficult to support a family."[249] Working conditions included twenty-four-hour days with "no toilet or lunch breaks," seventy-two consecutive-hour shifts in the high season, and crane workers—who are "not permitted to come down from the crane at all during the shift"—not only "have to eat meals in the 2m^2 space, but also are forced to solve the problem of bathroom visits here."[250]

The same calculations that ask workers to pee in bottles for reasons of productivity and efficiency (which is not a condition limited to the Hong Kong ports and has also been reported in Amazon warehouses in the West)[251] are in use, in different ways, in company after company, American and foreign alike. "These

247 Ellen David Friedman, "Hong Kong Dockworkers Strike Attracts Huge Solidarity," *Labor Notes*, last modified April 12, 2013, https://www.labornotes.org/2013/04/hong-kong-dockworkers-strike-attracts-huge-solidarity.

248 "I earn HK$15,000-$16,000 (US$2,000) during the high season, and less than HK$10,000 (US$1,300) for the low season."

249 Roland Lim, "Hong Kong Port Workers Threaten to Extend Strike," *Central News Asia*, last modified April 16, 2013, http://kapitanydv.ru/old/index.php?option=com_content&view=article&id=575:global-daily-news-17042013&catid=48:2010-07-04-07-01-09&Itemid=73.

250 Congyue Dai, "'All on the Same Ocean'—Hong Kong Dock Workers win 40-day Strike," *In Defense of Marxism*, last modified May 9, 2013, https://www.marxist.com/all-on-the-same-ocean-hong-kong-strike.htm.

251 Chris Pollard, "Amazon Workers Pee into Bottles to Save Time: Investigator," *New York Post*, last modified April 16, 2018, https://nypost.com/2018/04/16/amazon-warehouse-workers-pee-into-bottles-to-avoid-wasting-time-undercover-investigator/.

jobs suck," Erik Nieves from Plus One Robotics told me. In fact, he has a hashtag he uses to illustrate both the difficult nature of the jobs in question and the critical nature of the humans in the warehouse. Check out #robotsworkpeoplerule.

In 2011, Amazon paid Cetronia Ambulance Corps to station ambulances and paramedics at two of its Pennsylvania warehouses during a heat wave, following the collapse of workers in a 102-degree warehouse. Rather than temporarily halt or slow down production so as to install proper accommodations for the heat, Amazon paid the ambulances to stand by and eventually escort about fifteen people to nearby hospitals when they collapsed, and treated twenty or thirty more right there.[252] One of the emergency room doctors who saw the severity of these heat-related injuries called OSHA to report "an unsafe environment."[253] Following OSHA's resultant inspection, Amazon installed cooling units and fans, which one employee said was like "working in a convection oven while blow-drying your hair."[254]

Other Amazon warehouse employees describe physically demanding tasks needing to be done at such a pace that injury, often leading to a lifetime of pain and disability, is inevitable. The spaces themselves lack airflow, with a constant, maddening din of beeps and alarms.[255] In Mira Loma in 2013, workers at a warehouse primarily moving Walmart merchandise asked the state of California

---

252 David Streitfeld, "Inside Amazon's Very Hot Warehouse," *The New York Times*, September 19, 2011, https://bits.blogs.nytimes.com/2011/09/19/inside-amazons-very-hot-warehouse/.

253 Ibid.

254 Spencer Soper, "Inside Amazon's Warehouse," *The Morning Call*, last modified August 17, 2015, https://www.mcall.com/news/watchdog/mc-allentown-amazon-complaints-20110917-story.html.

255 Gaybrosaurus, "What It's Really like to Work in Amazon's Warehouse—Draining and Depressing—Undercover at Amazon: Exhausted Humans Are Inefficient so Robots Are Taking Over," Reddit, last modified November 27, 2017, https://www.reddit.com/r/Futurology/comments/7fvlr6/what_its_really_like_to_work_in_amazons_warehouse/.

to intervene to improve their working conditions, which included "blocked fire exits, frequent collapses of heavy boxes stacked 30 feet high, and lack of adequate drinking water." An employee reported "high stacks of boxes often [falling], and some of the forklifts don't have working brakes. We are often blocked inside of the metal shipping containers in the darkness."[256] Recent in the Mira Loma workers' minds was the Bangladeshi garment workers' fire, which killed more than 100 people. Since 2006, "more than 500 Bangladeshi workers have died in factory fires," fires which would have been easily avoidable had factories "taken the right precautions."[257]

WORKING HARDER, BUT NOT BETTER OFF

It is becoming increasingly difficult to tell the difference between efforts to maximize efficiency from a reckless flouting of workers' basic rights, let alone well-being. As two of the experts investing in and reporting on future technologies and their impacts on society, Davidow and Malone argue elsewhere in *The Autonomous Revolution*, rises in productivity that are linked to automation are no longer causing the economic expansion commonly associated with productivity booms. Rather than monetizable productivity—"improvements in productivity that significantly increased gross domestic product (GDP)"—automating technology has instead produced nonmonetizable productivity that "in many cases drive

---

256 "Warehouse Workers Exposed to Illegal and Dangerous Working Conditions Seek State Intervention," *Warehouse Worker Resource Center*, last modified May 23, 2013, http://www. warehouseworkers.org/warehouse-workers-exposed-to-illegal-and-dangerous-working-conditions-seek-state-intervention/.

257 Vikas Bajaj, "Fatal Fire in Bangladesh Highlights the Dangers Facing Garment Workers," *The New York Times*, last modified November 25, 2012, https://www.nytimes.com/2012/11/26/world/asia/bangladesh-fire-kills-more-than-100-and-injures-many.html.

GDP down instead of up."[258] The middle class—when and where it still exists—"is working better and smarter than it ever has, but it's not getting any wealthier."[259] This nonmonetizable productivity is due to the fact that the markets that automation and intelligent machines, as Davidow and Malone call them, affect are largely inelastic—when the price of a car dramatically decreased, for example, "sales increased by a factor of 200." But if the price of a newspaper "drops to near zero, people with limited time will not buy or read 100 times more news."[260]

PRODUCTIVITY WITHOUT PROSPERITY

"According to the economist Robert Gordon, US productivity grew at an annual rate of 2.82 percent between 1920 and 1970. During that same interval, GDP increased by more than 3.2 percent. When GDP grows faster than productivity, it generates a demand for more workers. Thus, the old productivity created not only more dollars of economic output but also jobs. Even more importantly, it created good times. Per capita GDP grew about 2 percent per year during that same half-century, and each generation earned about 50 percent more income than the one before. Workers' sons and daughters were almost certain to enjoy higher living standards than their parents."[261]

This is not to say that no one is getting wealthier; indeed, it's the exact opposite. As regulations have been globally rolled back, corporate profit margins have increased, as have concentrations of

258 William Davidow and Michael Malone, *The Autonomous Revolution: Reclaiming the Future We've Sold to Machines* (Oakland, CA: Berrett-Koehler Publishers, Inc., 2020).

259 Ibid.

260 Ibid.

261 Davidow and Malone, *The Autonomous Revolution*.

wealth. In 1965, the average CEO made twenty-four times more than the "average production worker, whereas in 2009, they made 185 times more."[262] As UC Berkeley economist Emmanuel Saez, among others, has found, income disparities have become so pronounced that by 2018, "America's top 10 percent now average more than nine times as much income as the bottom 90 percent. Americans in the top 1 percent tower stunningly higher. They average over 39 times more income than the bottom 90 percent. But that gap pales in comparison to the divide between the nation's top 0.1 percent and everyone else. Americans at this lofty level are taking in over 196 times the income of the bottom 90 percent."[263]

Even ignoring the larger economic trends borne out of blind adherence to productivity, it is easy to see how—specifically in relation to warehousing and the supply chain—the potential profits automation might enable can also come with significant losses, financial and otherwise. Workforce turnover is a huge problem for warehouses—along with industries like mining, construction, and hospitality. The warehouse workforce has one of the highest turnover rates.[264] In California, turnover rates for warehouse workers was 83 percent, up more than 40 points since 2011.[265] The National Employment Law Project found that the average turnover rate for warehouse workers "in counties with Amazon fulfillment centers was 100.9 percent in 2017," or, in other words,

262 "20 Facts About U.S. Inequality that Everyone Should Know," *Stanford Center on Poverty & Inequality*, last modified 2011, https://inequality.stanford.edu/publications/20-facts-about-us-inequality-everyone-should-know.

263 "Income Inequality in the United States," *Inequality.org, accessed October 12, 2020,* https://inequality.org/facts/income-inequality/.

264 "Annual Total Separations Rates by Industry and Region, Not Seasonally Adjusted," U.S. Bureau of Labor Statistics, last modified March 17, 2020, https://www.bls.gov/news.release/jolts.t16.htm.

265 Irene Tung and Deborah Berkowitz, "Amazon's Disposable Workers: High Injury and Turnover Rates at Fulfillment Centers in California," National Employment Law Project, last modified March 6, 2020, https://www.nelp.org/publication/amazons-disposable-workers-high-injury-turnover-rates-fulfillment-centers-california/.

"more workers leave their warehouse jobs each year than the total number of warehouse workers employed in those counties."[266] There is no doubt that these incredibly high turnover rates are a direct product of worker treatment and experience in these warehouses. One Amazon worker said the warehouse "is like a prison."[267]

TURNOVER COSTS ARE HIGH

Conservative estimates, based on an annual worker's salary of $28,000, put replacement costs for these vanishing workers at $7,000 per worker, or about 25 percent of the worker's salary.[268] Through expenditures such as "exit interviews, severance pay, increased unemployment taxes, overtime pay to replace lost time, temp staffing, additional advertising, recruitment fees, screening costs, drug testing, background checks, possible relocation costs, orientation training, certifications, uniforms, and informational literature,"[269] this number could easily balloon past $7,000.

In addition, the US Bureau of Labor Statistics recorded an uptick in warehouse fatalities between 2015 and 2018, as well as 5 per 100 illnesses or injuries, more than 50 percent higher than the industry-wide standard of 3.2 per 100.[270] These numbers reflect potential worker's compensation, disability, and litigation pay-

266 Ibid.

267 Pollard, "Amazon Workers Pee into Bottles."

268 Veronica Donchez, "Warehouse Labor: The 'Real' Cost of Warehouse Worker Turnover," *Kane Logistics*, last modified May 21, 2019, https://www.kaneisable.com/blog/warehouse-labor-the-real-cost-of-warehouse-worker-turnover.

269 Ibid.

270 Clare Condon, "Warehouse Worker Deaths and Injuries Higher than Average," *EHS Daily Advisor*, last modified December 7, 2017, https://ehsdailyadvisor.blr.com/2017/12/warehouse-worker-deaths-injuries-higher-average/.

ments that companies continuously make in response to their workplace environments. In 2018, *Vice* reported that "ambulances have been called to Amazon's UK warehouses at least 600 times in the last three years."[271] The company also faces ongoing lawsuits resulting from the firing of pregnant women,[272] unpaid wages, or wage theft,[273] discrimination against older and disabled workers,[274] and redactions in OSHA's Amazon injury records—just to name a few.[275]

That is all to say that the final, perhaps also nonmonetizable, cost of an unchecked allegiance to productivity is an ethical one. This, though, is beginning to have more and more of an impact on businesses—especially the huge ones—who are being asked to account for their behavior and socioeconomic, cultural, and environmental impacts. In 2019, Amazon's annual Prime Day saw protests across the country with people taking to the streets against Amazon's "labor practices and its involvement with US authorities' deportation efforts."[276] There is a growing movement to boycott Amazon with fairly straightforward business outlets publishing articles

271 Mark Wilding, "Ambulances Were Called to Amazon Warehouses 600 Times in Three Years," *Vice*, last modified May 31, 2018, https://www.vice.com/en_us/article/7xm4dy/ambulances-were-called-to-amazon-warehouses-600-times-in-three-years.

272 Zack Budryk, "Lawsuits Claimed Amazon Fired Pregnant Warehouse Workers who Asked for More Bathroom Breaks: Report," *The Hill*, last modified May 2, 2019, https://thehill.com/policy/technology/442595-seven-lawsuits-claimed-amazon-fired-pregnant-warehouse-workers-who-asked.

273 Hayley Peterson, "More than 200 Delivery Drivers Are Suing Amazon over Claims of Missing Wages," *Business Insider*, last modified September 13, 2018, https://www.businessinsider.com/amazon-delivery-drivers-claim-missing-wages-lawsuit-2018-9.

274 Patricia Cohen, "New Evidence of Age Bias in Hiring, and a Push to Fight It," *The New York Times*, last modified June 7, 2019, https://www.nytimes.com/2019/06/07/business/economy/age-discrimination-jobs-hiring.html.

275 Evans, "Ruthless Quotas."

276 Kari Paul, "Prime Day: Activists Protest against Amazon in Cities across US," *The Guardian*, last modified July 15, 2019, https://www.theguardian.com/technology/2019/jul/15/prime-day-activists-plan-protests-in-us-cities-and-a-boycott-of-e-commerce-giant.

like "Your complete guide to living an Amazon-free life in 2019."[277] In a leaked memo, top Amazon executives called a worker who was attempting to bring attention to Amazon's increasingly dangerous working conditions during the COVID-19 pandemic "not smart or articulate" and fired him for "violating social distancing guidelines and putting the safety of others at risk."[278] Condemnation was swift—from NYC mayor Bill de Blasio to Bernie Sanders, people decried Amazon's behavior, particularly against its employees who have continued to work in increasingly dangerous situations.[279]

Yet, people—more and more people—keep using Amazon. Indeed, one of this book's main arguments has been that smaller, independent companies must automate if they want to stay competitive in a market with customer expectations that have largely been created by Amazon and a couple of other major retailers and marketplaces. But, as we have also seen, without their economy of scale, it is next to impossible for other organizations to attempt to copy any of Amazon's business practices.

IT ISN'T A FAIR FIGHT

According to many analysts and insiders, this is, in fact, the point: Amazon has shifted the market as they have—at least in part—specifically to drive smaller, independent organizations out of business. It can be argued that Amazon has taken the practice of

---

277 Cale Guthrie Weissman, "Your Complete Guide to Living an Amazon-Free Life in 2019," *Fast Company*, last modified December 20, 2018, https://www.fastcompany.com/90281892/bezos-boycott-how-to-live-an-amazon-free-life.

278 Julia Carrie Wong, "Amazon Execs Labeled Fired Worker 'Not Smart or Articulate' in Leaked PR Notes," *The Guardian*, last modified April 2, 2020, https://www.theguardian.com/technology/2020/apr/02/amazon-chris-smalls-smart-articulate-leaked-memo.

279 Ben Fox Rubin and Sean Keane, "Amazon Fires Three Workers who Criticized Warehouse Conditions,"*cnet*, last modified April 14, 2020, https://www.cnet.com/news/amazon-fires-two-tech-workers-who-criticized-warehouse-conditions/.

predatory pricing (a "long-standing concept in economic thought [in which] to get the better of a competitor, a business drops the price of a product to below its cost to produce. The competitor, unable to beat the price, goes out of business. Then the company, now with a monopoly, raises prices, recouping the loss" and one for which Amazon is being investigated[280]) into every aspect of business, from product pricing, to shipping, to employee wages.

In his 2013 book, *The Everything Store: Jeff Bezos and the Age of Amazon,* Brad Stone documents that Amazon, at least in the very beginning, participated in normal, if heated, business competition. In 1996/1997, Amazon—then just a bookstore—found itself up against the brand-new online arm of Barnes & Noble, Barnesand-Noble.com. In stiff competition, "each [asserted] it had a better selection and lower prices. Barnes & Noble laid claim to a deeper catalog; Amazon ramped up efforts to track down books in independent bookshops and at antique-book dealers."[281] Though we all know who eventually won this battle, early competition seemed to stay inside the bounds of normalcy.

By 2009, however, any ideas of healthy competition seemed to be a thing of the company's past. Marc Lore and Vinit Bharara, co-founders of Diapers.com had built a thriving e-commerce company with a dedicated following of new parents, as well as a sophisticated distribution process. In their parent company, Quidsi's FC, Lore and Bharara "used software to match every order with the smallest possible box (there were twenty-three available), minimizing excess weight and thus reducing the per-order shipping cost. (Amazon, which had to match box sizes to a much larger

---

280 Colin Lecher, "How Low Prices Could Make for an Antitrust Case against Amazon," *The Verge*, last modified May 13, 2019, https://www.theverge.com/2019/5/13/18563379/amazon-predatory-pricing-antitrust-law.

281 Brad Stone, *The Everything Store: Jeff Bezos and the Age of Amazon* (New York: Little, Brown, 2013).

selection of products, was not as adept at this.)"[282] Once the duo had offered their customers the extremely popular subscription option for parenting staples, Amazon and other huge players had taken notice of Quidsi and Diapers.com.

Although "executives and official representatives from Amazon, Quidsi, and Walmart all declined to discuss the ensuing scuffle in detail," Amazon's mergers and acquisitions chief Jeff Blackburn told Stone that "everything Amazon subsequently did in the diapers market was planned beforehand and was unrelated to competing with Quidsi."[283] This seems hard to believe at best, as having rejected Amazon's overtures to buy them out, Lore and Bharara "noticed Amazon dropping prices up to 30 percent on diapers and other baby products. As an experiment, Quidsi execs manipulated their prices and then watched as Amazon's website changed its prices accordingly. Amazon's famous pricing bots were lasered in on Diapers.com."[284]

Amazon's entrance into the diaper market made outside investors weary and with Amazon's prices dropping their own sales, Quidsi responded to buyout advances from Walmart. When offered a less than satisfactory amount, they finally turned to Amazon. Flying to Seattle, Lore and Bharara met directly with Bezos. While in the meeting, Amazon released a press statement outlining its new program: "it was a sweet deal for new parents: they could get up to a year's worth of free two-day shipping...and there was a wealth of other perks available, including an additional 30 percent off the already-discounted diapers if they signed up for regular monthly deliveries of diapers as part of a service called Subscribe and

282 Ibid.

283 Ibid.

284 Ibid.

Save."[285] Quidsi employees couldn't reach the company's founders to discuss Amazon's move, as the two were, as mentioned, with Bezos. When Quidsi reckoned their information on the diaper industry with Amazon's prices, they calculated that Amazon was "on track to lose $100 million over three months in the diaper category alone."[286]

Completely trapped, Quidsi had no choice but to sell, and sell low, to Amazon. One month after acquiring Diapers.com, Amazon closed its Amazon Mom program to new members. After ongoing investigation from the FTC regarding the purchase, Amazon reopened Amazon Mom, though "with much smaller discounts." As there still existed other diaper merchants, Amazon wasn't found to be a monopoly. Bezos, as Stone says, "had won again."[287] Today, Amazon Mom is a thing of the past. Folded into Amazon Family, members have to have Prime accounts, which enable them to access further discounts on subscription items such as diapers. As for prices, as of May 2020, Amazon lists a 168-count pack of Pampers Swaddlers for $0.279 per unit. Over at Target the diapers cost $.027 per unit for the same product, no paid membership necessary.

From Bezos's Endless.com, designed to drive Zappos out of business, to less all-out assaults such as the Birkenstocks' story mentioned earlier, Diapers.com was not the first to face this type of ruthless treatment from Amazon. They're also not likely to be the last. According to various analysts, Amazon is primed (inevitable pun) to vastly change if not destroy several industries and many companies. To name just a few, these include the pharma-

---

285 Ibid.

286 Ibid.

287 Ibid.

ceutical industry, Walgreens, CVS, and Rite-Aid in particular, with Amazon's purchase of the online PillPack;[288] meal kit and delivery providers such as Blue Apron, HelloFresh, and Plated, with Amazon's acquisition of Whole Foods;[289] and Etsy, which cut 22 percent of its staff in 2017 as Amazon expanded its Handmade brand.[290]

As a *Nation* headline succinctly put it, "Amazon Doesn't Want to Just Dominate the Market—It Wants to Become the Market."[291] Amazon, the article argues, has been built to replace existing markets. Bezos's "vision is for Amazon to become the underlying infrastructure that commerce runs on."[292] Like I pointed out at the beginning of the book, Charles Duhigg's article in *The New Yorker*, "Is Amazon Unstoppable?" shows us the monolith has done this in a variety of ways, from shifting the nature of commerce itself to deciding who can sell what, when, and where.[293] This leaves many companies in the "if you can't beat 'em, join 'em" boat; many of Amazon's fiercest critics have become third-party sellers on the platform. What, if any, are the alternatives?

288 Aaron Hankin, "A Dozen or so Companies Amazon Is Slaying This Year," *Investopedia*, last modified June 25, 2019, https://www.investopedia.com/news/5-companies-amazon-killing/.

289 James Brumley, "43 Companies Amazon Could Destroy (Including One for a Second Time)," *Kiplinger*, last modified November 27, 2019, https://www.kiplinger.com/slideshow/investing/T052-S001-43-companies-amazon-amzn-could-destroy/index.html.

290 Aaron Hankin, "A Dozen or so Companies Amazon Is Slaying This Year."

291 Stacy Mitchell, "Amazon Doesn't Just Want to Dominate the Market—It Wants to Become the Market." *The Nation*, last modified February 15, 2018, https://www.thenation.com/article/archive/amazon-doesnt-just-want-to-dominate-the-market-it-wants-to-become-the-market/.

292 Ibid.

293 See, for example, the story of Amazon and Birkenstock in *The New Yorker*'s "Is Amazon Unstoppable?" by Charles Duhigg, last modified October 10, 2019, https://www.newyorker.com/magazine/2019/10/21/is-amazon-unstoppable, which is also summarized earlier in "The Copycats—Counterfeiting on Amazon" section.

JEFF BEZOS VS. JACK MA

In aspiring to become commerce's "underlying infrastructure," Bezos will, at some point, run into trouble in the form of Jack Ma, whose fellow Big 5 member, Alibaba, also aims to "build the future infrastructure of commerce."

THE WORK ENVIRONMENT

This book has argued that automation is key to survival—at the same time, this is not a process without potential repercussions. As Davidow and Malone have pointed out, "the technologies creating many of these problems can also be used to solve them."[294] Robotics, in particular, has fundamentally changed the literal and figurative value of some human labor, but this needn't be the end of the story. Worker treatment is, in fact, one of the few remaining areas of business in which companies can and must act differently than Amazon and its many predecessors and followers in the supply chain, not just because it's the right thing to do, but because it is also the best decision for long-term business prosperity, and, yes, productivity. Companies must broadcast to current and future customers how these efforts make them unique and why customers should care.

Yet, focusing on worker treatment in the warehouse rarely happens today. These are the habits more typical of companies who value and demand the intellectual and creative, rather than physical output of their employees. Company culture has become a catchphrase in the business world, often referencing the workplace environments of Silicon Valley, with their endless perks, like unlimited PTO, in-office happy hours, zen rooms, ping pong

---

294 Davidow and Malone, *The Autonomous Revolution.*

tables, and pet-friendly offices.[295] A commitment to the workplace environment is a must for companies hoping to attract and keep the young employees they seek, with "65% of 18-to-34-year-olds [likely] to place culture above salary."[296] Not only do such initiatives save organizations money by avoiding all those turnover losses mentioned above, they can also lead to increased productivity figures as workers are increasingly motivated to perform and contribute.

Though the startup ethos might not be a direct fit for warehouses, the current working environment leaves plenty of room for improvement as it is often downright hostile to its human employees. Down to the level of design, warehouses have not been envisioned as human spaces—though once built without windows through consideration for insulation and stock, now even skylights are being covered, because the "glare might throw off the machines' sensors."[297] The psychological impacts of these spaces are as huge as they are unquantifiable. Numerous Amazon employees have reported severe depression and suicidal thinking, with one former warehouse worker telling *Vox*: "[Y]ou spend ten hours on foot, there's no windows in the place, and you're not allowed to talk to people—there's no interactions allowed. I got a sense in no time at all that they work people to death, or until they get too tired to keep working. I felt I couldn't work there and maintain a healthy state of mind."[298]

295 "Culture Matters: How Great Startups Will Thrive In 2020," *Forbes*, last modified February 11, 2020, https://www.forbes.com/sites/ellevate/2020/02/11/culture-matters-how-great-startups-will-thrive-in-2020/#299641b57c76.

296 Ibid.

297 Matt Simon, "Inside the Amazon Warehouse Where Humans and Machines Become One," *Wired*, last modified June 5, 2019,https://www.wired.com/story/amazon-warehouse-robots/.

298 Chavie Lieber, "Suicide Attempts and Mental Breakdowns: 911 Calls from Amazon Warehouses Reveal that Some Workers Are Struggling," *Vox*,last modified March 11, 2019, https://www.vox.com/the-goods/2019/3/11/18260472/amazon-warehouse-workers-911-calls-suicide.

Automation forces companies to evaluate how they conceptualize the role of labor, and the market will soon force them to evaluate why they conceptualize it as they do. The increasing automation of many warehouse jobs could potentially afford companies with the ability to upskill a large chunk of their labor force, as well as pay those whose as-is jobs continue to be essential for a better wage with benefits. In fact, this is another place where Big Data can be put to use in pinpointing the most beneficial ways a given company could upskill its workers, while also assessing ROI per employee, per program, and so on.[299] As automation drastically reduces the number while simultaneously changing the parameters of what is considered a good job (long the hallmark of American class mobility), companies must consider their roles in this new economic future. If, as a 2013 study by Frey and Osborne predicts, "47 percent of American jobs might be automated in the future,"[300] there is a huge opportunity here to positively reconsider the role and worth of human labor. Just as the longshoremen spread around the profits produced by the shipping container's greater efficiency, so too could warehouses concerned with a better quality of life and work for its employees share the wealth. Given the high cost of replacing workers and caring for those with injuries, the data may soon show that investing in warehouse worker well-being is actually good for business and the bottom line.

The belief, either explicit or implied, in the inherent disposability of this type of labor has tremendous societal impacts outside of business' bottom lines. Excluding circumstances brought about by COVID-19, the US has been experiencing record-low unemploy-

---

299 Daniel Newman, "4 Key Practices For Upskilling Workers In The Age of Digital Transformation," *Forbes*, last modified July 25, 2018, https://www.forbes.com/sites/danielnewman/2018/07/25/4-key-practices-for-upskilling-workers-in-the-age-of-digital-transformation/#7934437a1a3e.

300 Carl Benedikt Frey and Michael A. Osborne, "The Future of Employment: How Susceptible Are Jobs to Computerisation?" Oxford Martin School, University of Oxford, last modified September 17, 2013, https://www.oxfordmartin.ox.ac.uk/downloads/academic/The_Future_of_Employment.pdf.

ment, a trend driven by lower "entry rates into unemployment, both from employment and from OLF (out of the labor force), likely due to population aging, better quality matches between workers and jobs, and other structural factors."[301] These lower entry rates into unemployment, however, do not exist in labor associated with the supply chain, where packers and packagers average 9.7 percent unemployment; weighers, measurers, checkers and the like 8.4; laborers and freight, stock, and material movers 7.7; while those in the agricultural sector often suffer from higher than one in ten unemployment rates.[302] The wealth disparities of which these numbers are an indication "touch nearly every aspect of daily lives, from career prospects and educational opportunities to health risks and neighborhood safety."[303] Not only that—as Supreme Court Justice Louis Brandeis said, "[W]e can either have democracy in this country or we can have great wealth concentrated in the hands of a few, but we can't have both."[304]

ARE HIGHER WAGES AND BENEFITS GOOD FOR BUSINESS?

Many of the suggestions in this section cost real dollars, dollars that are desperately needed for other automations. We've read that replacing highly repetitive, difficult tasks with hardware, robotics,

301 Marianna Kudlyak and Mitchell G. Ochse, "Why is Unemployment Currently So Low?" *Federal Reserve Bank of San Francisco*, last modified March 2, 2020, https://www.frbsf.org/economic-research/publications/economic-letter/2020/march/why-is-unemployment-currently-so-low/.

302 Samuel Stebbins, "Jobs with the Best and Worst Security Based on Unemployment Rate," *USA Today*, last modified March 6, 2019, https://www.usatoday.com/story/money/careers/2019/03/06/unemployment-rate-2019-occupations-best-worst-job-security/39124227/.

303 Christina Pazzanese, "The Costs of Inequality: Increasingly, It's the Rich and the Rest," *The Harvard Gazette*, last modified February 8, 2016, https://news.harvard.edu/gazette/story/2016/02/the-costs-of-inequality-increasingly-its-the-rich-and-the-rest/.

304 Ibid.

and software should reduce the total number of employees needed to run an operation, but that people are still imperative. At this point, those savings should be invested in worker wage increases and benefits whenever possible. Doing so may increase profitability by reducing turnover and its associated costs, improving employee engagement, output, and each worker's investment in the business' success.

If you don't want to take my word for it, consider some real-world examples operating in plain sight. A great illustration of why investing in worker well-being is a good idea comes from the fiercely competitive world of fast food. California-based burger chain, In-N-Out, which operates only about 350 locations,[305] competes head-to-head with massive competitors like Subway (over 41,000 locations),[306] McDonalds (over 37,000 locations),[307] Burger King (over 17,000 locations),[308] and Taco Bell (over 7,000 locations).[309] As of this writing, In-N-Out charges only $2.10 for a hamburger and $1.60 for fries, prices that since 1989, have not even kept up with inflation.[310] Yet an In-N-Out worker's starting wage is over $13 per hour, $3 to $4 higher than the national average of their competitors,[311] and comes with a career path to a store

305 "In-N-Out Burger," Wikipedia, accessed July 16, 2020, https://en.wikipedia.org/wiki/
    In-N-Out_Burger.

306 "Subway (restaurant)," Wikipedia, accessed July 16, 2020, https://en.wikipedia.org/wiki/
    Subway_(restaurant).

307 "McDonald's," Wikipedia, accessed July 19, 2020, https://en.wikipedia.org/wiki/McDonald's.

308 "Burger King," Wikipedia, accessed July 14, 2020, https://en.wikipedia.org/wiki/Burger_King.

309 "Taco Bell," Wikipedia, accessed July 10, 2020, https://en.wikipedia.org/wiki/Taco_Bell.

310 "The Snyder Family made IN-N-OUT BURGER," *Investment Master Class*, last
    modified December 3, 2018, http://mastersinvest.com/newblog/2018/10/21/
    learning-from-lynsi-snyder-in-n-out-burger.

311 Ibid.

management position that pays $160,000, and doesn't require a college degree.[312]

Much like warehouse work, this is not an easy job, evidenced by an employee's Glassdoor review detailing a "fast-paced environment" with "very hard" work and "no shortcuts." In spite of these higher wages, or more likely, in part, because of them, as of 2018, "[a]n In-N-Out store outsells a typical McDonald's nearly twice over, bringing in an estimated $4.5 million in gross annual sales versus McDonald's $2.6 million. (In-N-Out, which is private, won't comment on its financials.) In-N-Out's profit margin (measured by earnings before interest, taxes, depreciation, and amortization) is an estimated 20 percent. That's higher than In-N-Out's East Coast rival Shake Shack (16 percent) and other restaurant chains that typically own their locations, like Chipotle (10.5 percent)."[313]

These are not isolated results. Chick-Fil-A employs similar wage policies and sees near-identical results, averaging $4.7 million in sales per store in 2018.[314] Remember, Chick-Fil-A realizes these numbers even though they are closed on Sundays.

In addition, both operations' employee turnover rate is historically below those of their competitors.[315] In an industry in which

312 Josh Hafner, "In-N-Out Managers Make $160,000 per Year," *USA Today*, last modified January 26, 2018, https://www.usatoday.com/story/money/nation-now/2018/01/25/n-out-mangers-make-160-000-per-year-reports-show/1065434001/.

313 Chloe Sorvino, "Exclusive: In-N-Out Billionaire Lynsi Snyder Opens Up About her Troubled Past And The Burger Chain's Future," *Forbes*, last modified October 10, 2018, https://www.forbes.com/sites/chloesorvino/2018/10/10/exclusive-in-n-out-billionaire-lynsi-snyder-opens-up-about-her-troubled-past-and-the-burger-chains-future/#49c6c75b4b9c.

314 Evie Liu, "McDonald's and Other Fast Food Chains Should Keep an Eye on Chick-Fil-A," *Barron's*, last modified June 10, 2019, https://www.barrons.com/articles/mcdonalds-has-a-real-competitor-in-chick-fil-a-51560162600.

315 Emily Schmall, "The Cult of Chick-fil-A," *Forbes*, last modified July 6, 2007, https://www.forbes.com/forbes/2007/0723/080.html#1b8304d45971.

near 100 percent or greater turnover rates are the norm, this is more difficult than it seems.[316] As Saru Jayaraman, UC Berkeley's Food Labor Research Center's lead, says, In-N-Out's considerable benefits and retention strategies aren't the company "performing charity—a loyal workforce means increased productivity, less employee turnover, and in the long run, larger profits."[317]

HIGHER PAY MEANS HIGHER PROFITS

Before the COVID-19 pandemic, many people saw operations labor as disposable. Now, these truck drivers, delivery workers, packers, sorters, and materials movers are regularly called heroes (follow #heroclass), and their labor is thought of as undeniably essential. In late May 2020, Target released its earnings report, citing a 141 percent growth in digital sales. Previous to the report, Target CEO Brian O'Connell stated that the two-dollar-per-hour COVID-19 wage increase would extend through July 4, with the company also continuing to "waive fees and charges for its backup daycare program, while also extending paid leave for workers who are 65 and older, have underlying medical conditions, or who are pregnant."[318] Though such expenditures undoubtedly cut into the company's earnings, Target's press release stated that "[W]ith our stores at the center of our strategy, and a significant investment in the safety of our team and guests, our operations had the

---

316 Eric Rosenbaum, "Panera Is Losing Nearly 100% of its Workers Every Year as Fast-Food Turnover Crisis Worsens," *CNBC*, last modified August 29, 2019, https://www.cnbc.com/2019/08/29/fast-food-restaurants-in-america-are-losing-100percent-of-workers-every-year.html.

317 Loren Feldman, "Today's Must-Reads For Entrepreneurs: Why In-N-Out Burger Pays Store Managers $160,000 A Year," *Forbes*, last modified February 12, 2018, https://www.forbes.com/sites/lorenfeldman/2018/02/12/human-resources-trade-wages-retail/#23d6ff9b5d6a.

318 Scott Van Voorhis, "Target Extends Pandemic Pay Boost as Earnings Loom," TheStreet, last modified May 18, 2020, https://www.thestreet.com/investing/target-coronavirus-pandemic-pay-boost-tgt-earnings.

agility and flexibility needed to meet the changing needs of our business."[319]

People outside the supply chain are also beginning to understand just how interrelated the global economy has become. Investing in workers will extend this thinking with the newly added awareness that our businesses are dependent on intricately linked markets of all kinds. Then, perhaps we can remember that though this labor was not called heroic yesterday, it should continue to be called as such tomorrow.

QUICK TAKEAWAYS

1. The COVID-19 pandemic brought to light the vital nature of operations workers.
2. Income disparities are larger than ever. Productivity improvements by way of automation are frequently non-monetizable, meaning workers are working harder, but they aren't getting wealthier by doing so.
3. Worker turnover is a huge problem, exceeding 100 percent in some areas. Turnover comes at a significant cost to the workers and to the bottom line.
4. Many companies improved wages and benefits in the midst of COVID-19 due to the essential nature of operations workers. Some plan to discontinue the benefits; others are here to stay. Real results of improved workers' treatment remain to be seen.

319 "Target Corporation Reports First Quarter Earnings," Target, last modified May 20, 2020, https://investors.target.com/news-releases/news-release-details/target-corporation-reports-first-quarter-earnings.

5. An unchecked allegiance to productivity comes at a cost, and businesses must act differently than the giants and their followers in the supply chain, not just because it's the right thing to do, but because it is also the best decision for long-term business prosperity and productivity.

CASE STUDY

See how companies are making operations employees key drivers of their business models and success in the Parker Clay and Shinesty Case Studies in Appendix A.

PART 3

I'M A HUSTLER, BABY

CHAPTER 13

THE FUTURE OF OUR COMMUNITIES

The epochal transformation we are witnessing is coming at a huge cost. Reckless driving and speeding are now commonplace in residential neighborhoods and will get worse as more companies fight for delivery promise parity. Marketplace piracy and counterfeiting have exploded, leaving small businesses with little to show for their inventions or ingenuity. Packing materials continue to gobble up billions of trees and fill our landfills and waterways with mass quantities of plastic. Businesses continue to exploit and damage human workers so they can deliver faster and faster and faster.

A 2014 *Atlantic* article titled "Is 'Progress' Good for Humanity?" points out that "[t]o criticize industrial modernity is somehow to criticize the moral advancement of humankind since a central theme in this narrative is the idea that industrialization revolutionized our humanity, too. Those who criticize industrial society are often met with defensive snarkiness: 'So you'd like us to go back to living in caves, would ya?' or 'You can't stop progress!'"[320]

---

320 Jeremy Caradonna, "Is 'Progress' Good for Humanity?" *The Atlantic*, last modified September 9, 2014, https://www.theatlantic.com/business/archive/2014/09/the-industrial-revolution-and-its-discontents/379781/.

Given the negative human and environmental factors derived from these *advancements*—better-termed *conveniences*—it is reasonable for business leaders to ask, "Is the juice worth the squeeze?" when making decisions for their businesses.

"The societal phase changes of the past enabled us to gain control over the natural world, create civilizations, and live comfortable and meaningful lives. But those achievements came at the cost of great human suffering."[321]

A successful future requires us to "rethink the narrative of progress" as "the simple-minded narrative of progress needs to be rethought."[322]

AUTOMATION'S NEXT PHASE—PREDICTIONS

Here are eight predictions for automation's next phase, some of which have the potential to improve the world for our children and theirs:

1. **Neighborhood optimization.** Amazon's next-day and same-day deliveries get a lot of attention, but a lesser publicized service called Amazon Day tells us more about where the market is moving. When it comes to the final-mile problem, density is key. Carriers want to make as many deliveries as close together as possible. Amazon is no different. Consolidating deliveries doesn't just help with reducing deliveries throughout the week; it improves density on those days. More packages for fewer stops.

2. **Amazon is not the only company working to improve den-**

---

321 William Davidow and Michael Malone, *The Autonomous Revolution: Reclaiming the Future We've Sold to Machines*, (Oakland, CA: Berrett-Koehler Publishers, Inc., 2020).

322 Caradonna, "Is 'Progress' Good for Humanity?"

sity. Shipping carriers like FedEx and UPS want the same thing. To be clear, the goal isn't to become the US Postal Service and stop at every house, every day. The goal is to drive down costs as low as possible. The best way to do this is fewer stops spaced closer together.

3. **Manufacturing will move closer to the final mile.** Predictive data, 3D printing, improvements in inventory availability and accuracy, ship from store, and other advancements will continue to move the manufacturing and positioning of many items closer to their final destinations. We may see the proliferation of regional assembling facilities who receive and assemble parts into finished goods for final delivery.

4. **3D printing.** Since its inception, 3D printing has promised big advancements, but in reality, it's been more of a novelty as it's seen as slow, expensive, and effective with few materials. That all changed with COVID-19. "The pandemic has illuminated these opportunities and obstacles, showing businesses that there's value in building the kinds of distributed supply chains that 3D printing promises..."[323] When the global supply chain broke, and people were desperate for respirators, masks, and other hard-to-find items, HP "spun up a COVID-19 task force, mobilizing a global effort to design and manufacture products that could be printed on its industrial-size machines" and subsequently, alongside their partners, delivered "1.5 million 3D-printed parts for ventilators, CPAP respirators, face shields, masks, and other devices."[324] Despite the amazing YouTube videos on the subject, I'm not predicting mass adoption of 3D printed homes anytime soon, but I do believe

323 Mike Murphy, "3D Printing Finally Found its Market, and All It Took Was a Pandemic," Protocol, last modified May 5, 2020, https://www.protocol.com/3d-printing-found-market-in-coronavirus-pandemic.

324 Ibid.

manufacturing solutions like 3D printing and inventories will continue to move closer to the home.

5. **Inside the home delivery.** In 2018, Amazon acquired Ring, the company famous for its video doorbells. As the media was getting excited, "Amazon's $1 billion acquisition of the doorbell-camera startup, Ring is the company doing what it does best—and it should terrify every other retailer."[325] The future was changing, and the Big 5 now had another key to unlock a previously impenetrable fortress. Shortly after the Ring acquisition, Walmart "announced a new service called InHome Delivery that allows customers to order groceries from Walmart's website and have them delivered directly to their fridge."[326] Whether it's groceries that must remain cold, furniture that needs to be set up, or a neighborhood full of porch pirates who don't mind the occasional glitter bomb, the Big 5 will be sending their workers into your home soon— unless, of course, they are already there.

6. **Carrier services will continue to be commoditized.** There will be less emphasis on the color of a carrier's truck and more on capacity availability, data accessibility, technology integrations, same-day and next-day service offerings, and performance. Smaller carriers may be disadvantaged globally but may find easier wins in local regions where they can more easily find density. We are already seeing successes by same-day providers in high-density environments like San Francisco, New York, and Seattle. These companies may never be able to compete in less-dense suburban and rural areas. Of course, once an advantage has been established, the big carri-

---

325 Dennis Green, "Amazon's $1 Billion Acquisition of the Doorbell-Camera Startup Ring Is the Company Doing What It Does Best—and It Should Terrify Every Other Retailer," *Business Insider*, last modified March 3, 2018, https://www.businessinsider.com/why-amazon-acquired-ring-2018-3.

326 Michael Grothaus, "Walmart Will Now Deliver Groceries to Your Fridge," *Fast Company*, last modified October 15, 2019, https://www.fastcompany.com/90417463/walmart-will-now-deliver-groceries-to-your-fridge.

ers will come calling, looking to change the color of the trucks and logos on their uniforms. The Big 5 will continue to fight to get bigger.

7. **Supply chain components will be key to differentiating business models.** Ikea's purchase of TaskRabbit, a same-day service platform that connects people with Taskers who can perform errands and odd-jobs for in-home furniture assembly is a great example. Whether 3D printing and local cross-docks support regional assembly or whether these services make their way directly to each buyer's home, auxiliary services will become more integrated with the independent brand's differentiation. If the past is any indication, the Big 5 will copy as many of them as possible, which will further the pace of independent innovation and reduce its value to humanity by way of the outsized human and environmental costs and lack of net positive economic value.

8. **Packaging form factor changes.** Over the past few decades, we have seen the wasteful ballooning of packaging designed to draw buyers' attention to products on shelves. We have all fought the anger-inducing battle of trying to open heat-sealed blister packs to get at the items we purchased. Believe it or not, there is even a term for the pain we experience when confronting this type of packaging: wrap rage or package rage.

Although eye-catching packaging is not going away anytime soon, retailers and manufacturers will continue to seek material and cost efficiencies by designing and utilizing simpler packaging. Companies like Grove Collaborative, an e-commerce retailer of eco-friendly home and beauty products, are already capitalizing on the efficiencies available to those willing to use less product and produce less waste by designing packaging for shipping. Remember the story about the Norelco packaging? For Amazon customers, Norelco reduced its complex thirteen packaging pieces to one simple brown box.[327]

This trend will continue and, in some cases, may even replace fancy packaging on store shelves as consumers continue prioritizing the reduction of their footprint.

Read more about Grove Collaborative in Appendix A.

1. **Expansion of ethical business models/components.** Purpose-driven business models will continue to grow in number and complexity, making it harder for copycats. We know the familiar stories of Tesla, TOMS shoes, and Method cleaning products. A Deloitte study found that the benefits of driving purpose into a business are significant. "Unilever's 28 'sustainable living' brands (i.e., brands focused on reducing Unilever's environmental footprint and increasing social impact) such as Dove, Vaseline, and Lipton delivered 75 percent of the company's growth and grew 69 percent faster on average than the rest of its businesses in 2018 (compared to 46 percent in 2017). Soap, petroleum jelly, and tea are everyday household essentials, but by promoting sustainable living, these products became differentiated as they embody the company's purpose."[328]

The study found that "Purpose-oriented companies have higher productivity and growth rates, along with a more satisfied workforce who stay longer with them." As if those benefits

327 Laura Stevens and Erica E. Phillips, "Amazon Puzzles Over the Perfect Fit—in Boxes," *The Wall Street Journal*, last modified December 20, 2017, https://www.wsj.com/articles/amazon-aims-for-one-box-fits-all-1513765800.

328 Diana O'Brien, Andy Main, Suzanne Kounkel, and Anthony R. Stephan, "Purpose Is Everything," *Deloitte*, last modified October 15, 2019, https://www2.deloitte.com/us/en/insights/topics/marketing-and-sales-operations/global-marketing-trends/2020/purpose-driven-companies.html.

weren't enough, "...such companies report 30 percent higher levels of innovation and 40 percent higher levels of workforce retention than their competitors."[329] Are you seeing a theme here? These companies show that treating people and the planet with respect is not a separate agenda from making money. In fact, it can be a path to a faster-growing, more profitable enterprise. We can only hope that more of these models gain traction in commoditized goods.

2. **Heightened awareness around treatment of labor/workers.** Perhaps the most important change will be a heightened awareness and willingness to correct the treatment of warehouse and supply chain workers. The biggest catalyst for this movement will have been the COVID-19 outbreak, which brought the supply chain workers' immense value into the global spotlight. A *Washington Post* article titled "Warehouse workers are essential. It's time we treated them that way," correctly stated that "[t]hese people keep the country running—and serve as stewards for the population's health too, as many vulnerable people order groceries, medical devices, and other essential items through Amazon and its competitors. Without their labor, the economy skids to a halt."[330]

    This will have such broad-reaching implications that an exhaustive list of predictions is impossible to imagine, but at the very least, the warehouse environment, worker rights, and overall appreciation will all benefit from the added attention.

Our neighborhoods are the new frontier. They will see more trucks,

---

329 Ibid.

330 Alex Press, "Warehouse workers are essential. It's time we treated them that way." *The Washington Post*, last modified April 25, 2020, https://www.washingtonpost.com/outlook/2020/04/25/warehouse-workers-are-essential-its-time-we-treated-them-that-way/.

more traffic, and more packaging-waste issues. Although the dollar costs of goods may continue to drop, the real costs of piecemeal, residential deliveries at the click of a button will continue to grow.

Entrepreneurs and investors will be paying close attention. Santosh Sankar, founding partner of Dynamo Ventures, a supply chain and mobility venture capital fund, believes "warehouse automation investments will accelerate as supply chain leaders reevaluate their operations to allow for greater antifragility, operational efficiencies, and positioning during the next expansionary cycle."

CHAPTER 14

BACK TO THE BIG 5

A buddy of mine, Michael Perry, a hard-driving entrepreneur who lived the life of grinding through VC fundraising and product-market-fit challenges that accompany a young startup, was (and is) just as passionate about the independent merchant as I am, and he built a business to prove it. When he went looking for the best distribution channel, he settled on Shopify. Shopify is great at attracting partners who are equally committed to supporting independent merchants. When Michael ended up selling his company to Shopify, their chief marketing officer said as much when he told a *Venture Beat* reporter covering the acquisition that "Their vision of the future is squarely aligned with ours."[331]

Michael's company was Kit, an AI marketing assistant. "Kit can email your customers, build Facebook ads, sponsor Instagram photos, and send you timely reports to let you know if you sold those last ten pairs of designer jeans." In addition, "It can now help you set discounts, retarget website visitors, engage with the

---

331 Stewart Rogers, "Shopify Acquires Kit, the Artificially Intelligent Marketing Bot," *Venture Beat*, last modified April 13, 2016, https://venturebeat.com/2016/04/13/ shopify-acquires-kit-the-artificially-intelligent-marketing-bot/.

customer after an abandoned cart, and handle 404 errors—all through a simple chat interface..."[332]

Yes, this was Shopify investing in conversational commerce, but more importantly, the Kit acquisition was proof of Shopify investing in its smallest sellers. The genius behind Kit was that it helped new Shopify sellers make their first sales. Those who didn't yet understand how to drive traffic were thrilled to have a bot take over via simple, conversational text messages. When the first sales started rolling in, sellers became more confident and more dependent on the Shopify ecosystem. At the same time, they are also more successful in their capacity as independent merchants. "Shopify is the ideal company to acquire Kit," said Perry after the acquisition, who has now retired as the director of Kit for Shopify and is working on a new startup. "Their commitment to business owners and their view of the future is directly aligned with our own mission and goals. We both want small business owners and entrepreneurs to be successful."[333]

Before we get into the specific actions your business should consider, we need to come back to Shopify's place in the Big 5. I'm going to call out the trolls right up front: this is not an advertorial for Shopify. Just as I used the data to show Amazon's track record with their marketplace sellers, so too, I've presented the data behind Shopify's power. From the perspective of a modern-day retailer, manufacturer, or distributor, theirs just reads a bit...better.

In fact, Shopify has been called "the anti-Amazon."[334] According

332 Ibid.

333 Ibid.

334 Elizabeth Segran, "Shopify, on a Quest to Be the Anti-Amazon, Now Has 1 Million Businesses," *Fast Company*, last modified November 4, 2019, https://www.fastcompany.com/90426269/shopify-on-a-quest-to-be-the-anti-amazon-now-has-1-million-businesses.

to their Global Economic Impact Report, "By supporting over one million businesses," Shopify is "empowering the unique individuals behind them, and fostering more competition, [spreading] economic prosperity—from business owners to their families to communities and beyond. Together, [Shopify is] changing the face of commerce for good."[335]

Remember, each member of the Big 5 has a different relationship with the future. While the data suggests that some members of the Big 5 may not have humanity's best interests at heart while others do, Shopify's track record definitely puts them in the friend category. In fact, Shopify may be the independent merchants' only hope.

SHOPIFY'S PLACE IN THE BIG 5

Shopify's mission is to "make commerce better for everyone, so businesses can focus on what they do best: building and selling their products."[336] To prove this, it is also important to look at how they invest. The sheer number of tools on their products page is overwhelming. As you read through the list, it is clear that the Shopify team has taken great strides to understand the challenges facing today's independent merchants, and they've created a toolkit juggernaut to ensure their success. From business name generation and logo creation to sales tax automation, drop-ship support, and one-click order fulfillment, these examples don't begin to illustrate the breadth of resources available.

335 "Commerce: a Force for Good," Shopify, accessed October 12, 2020, https://cdn.shopify.com/static/impact-report/shopify-global-economic-impact-report-summary.pdf.

336 Isabelle Kirkwood, "Shopify's Lynsey Thornton Talks Mission-Driven Decisions at Traction 2019," betakit, last modified August 13, 2019, https://betakit.com/shopifys-lynsey-thornton-talks-mission-driven-decisions-at-traction-2019/.

In the future, I predict where the Big 5 could own global commerce—intention becomes everything—and I believe Shopify's past and present investments make their motives clear.

Shopify hasn't just invested in smaller sellers. Shopify Plus is its e-commerce platform investment in larger shippers, which Shopify defines as selling $1 million to $500 million annually. These include medium and enterprise-level customers like Staples, Lindt Chocolate, Marshawn Lynch's brand Beast Mode, Chubbies, and one of my favorites, Laird Superfood.[337]

There are two main sides to any marketplace: the eyeballs of the shoppers looking to buy, and the distribution or supply chain that gets the purchases into the buyers' hands. We all know that most people are now skipping Google and going straight to Amazon to search for products. In light of this behavior shift, these independent Shopify sellers, some of whom do sell some products on a variety of marketplaces (including Amazon), are part of a comprehensive sales strategy. They continue to report improvements in engagement, significant sales increases, all-time sales records, and seamless wholesale and retail channel management on a system that is not a direct threat to their livelihood or long-term viability. My friends, Ian and Brittany Bentley, founders of handcrafted lifestyle goods company, Parker Clay (a mission-driven company with insane growth that I encourage you to read about in Appendix A) told me plainly, "We couldn't have scaled the way we have without Shopify." (I encourage you to go to https://www.shopify.com/plus/customers and read the customer testimonials for yourself.)

Shopify's most recent acquisition of 6 River Systems is an enterprise-caliber investment that will give a major boost to all

---

337 "Find Out Why the World's Best Brands Choose Shopify Plus," Shopify, accessed October 12, 2020, https://www.shopify.com/plus/customers.

shippers on the Shopify Fulfillment Network, "a powerful and trusted fulfillment network that will ensure timely deliveries, lower shipping costs, and provide superb customer experience for merchants and their customers."[338]

This quote from Shopify's acquisition press release makes their intentions clear. "With the acquisition of 6 River Systems, Shopify will add a team with decades of experience in fulfillment software and robotics, including experienced leaders from Kiva Systems (now Amazon Robotics). Adding 6 River Systems' cloud-based software and collaborative mobile robots called "Chuck" to the Shopify Fulfillment Network will increase the speed and reliability of warehouse operations by empowering on-site associates with daily tasks, including inventory replenishment, picking, sorting, and packing."[339]

Remember RaaS (Robots-as-a-Service)? It exists to lower the entry point of robotics and the efficiencies that can be gained—if only it can be afforded. That is precisely what Shopify is doing: lowering the barrier to entry. By aggregating merchant volumes under one fulfillment umbrella, it seems clear that they are hoping to distribute Big 5 shipping power throughout their entire ecosystem.

Independents need Shopify to lead in this field more than they might know. Returning to Erik Nieves's idea of "the 94," it is important to note, as he does, that robotics—in addition to being one of smaller merchants' best strategies for self-preservation— also needs a champion within the market itself. A champion, that is, who doesn't keep their technology secret and unavailable. "In the automotive industry," says Nieves, "robotics did not take off

---

338 "Shopify to Acquire 6 River Systems," Shopify September 9, 2019, accessed October 12, 2020, https://news.shopify.com/shopify-to-acquire-6-river-systems.

339 Ibid

until GM said 'I'm all in. Not only am I all in, I'm going to require that my tier-one suppliers get on board.' And that is effectively what launched the industrial robotics market in the Americas." Without a company leading the way, such a revolution would have been impossible, Nieves argues. "The rest of the industry was waiting for somebody to say, 'This really works!' And once GM did, everybody else fell in line over the next 10 to 15 to 20 years. And now you don't do automotive without robots." The same type of vision and leadership is necessary now. Walmart is strong enough to fill this void, but given their struggles with e-commerce, it is unlikely they will. For the sake of independents everywhere, let's hope that Shopify, with 6 River Systems, steps into this leadership role.

ALIBABA, TENCENT, AND JD.COM

Of the Big 5 e-commerce powerhouses, this book focuses on those with the most influence on American businesses, namely Amazon and Walmart. However, as markets become increasingly globalized, such nationally defined borders are becoming more and more obsolete. Although companies like Alibaba, Tencent, and JD.com might not be household names right now, it is only a matter of time.

Aside from geographical distance, one of the reasons for this relative lack of US presence has to do with what might be considered a historical aspect of these companies' respective markets. As China has rapidly modernized its economy to compete in global capitalism, it has, in many ways, remained culturally and politically communist, if only in name. In an article on China's social credit system, Mara Hvistendahl notes that "there is not yet a great American super app" akin to the Chinese Alipay or WeChat. As she shows, these super apps harvest a tremendous amount of data about their users. While American companies surely do the same, their reach is not nearly as thorough, nor are their motivations necessarily the same. Whereas—at least for the time being—US data brokers mainly work to "better target ads," the same efforts in China are used to "exert social control."[340] As Jack Ma, founder of behemoth Alibaba said to *Fortune*, "This is the thing that drives me and so many of my associates: We always want to do good things for society."[341]

Whether or not it's *good* for society is open to debate. Alibaba is an inarguably huge presence in China and elsewhere. With a market capitalization of well over half a trillion US dollars as of June 12, 2020,[342] Alibaba originated as a B2B venture, whose "initial goal was to leverage the power of the wholesale internet marketplace."[343] Though this business aspect of Alibaba still exists, housed under Alibaba.com, as of year-end 2018, the entirety of Alibaba Group's offerings controlled an estimated "60% of the entire Chinese e-commerce market."[344] Along with Alibaba.com, Alibaba Group also owns Taobao, a business-to-consumer and consumer-to-consumer marketplace, and Tmall, which provides "literal authenticity for Chinese shoppers, [and] also acts as a conduit between foreign brands and Chinese shoppers."[345] By the end

340 Mara Hvistendahl, "Inside China's Vast New Experiment in Social Ranking," *Wired*, last modified December 14, 2017, https://www.wired.com/story/age-of-social-credit/.

341 Adam Lashinsky, "Alibaba v. Tencent."

342 "Alibaba Market Cap 2011-2019 | BABA," Macrotrends, accessed October 12, 2020, https://www.macrotrends.net/stocks/charts/BABA/alibaba/market-cap.

343 Brian O'Connell, "History of Alibaba: Timeline and Facts," TheStreet, last modified January 2, 2020, https://www.thestreet.com/world/history-of-alibaba-15145103.

344 Ibid.

345 Tatiana Walk-Morris, "What is it about Tmall?" Retail Dive, last modified September 19, 2019, https://www.retaildive.com/news/what-is-it-about-tmall/562907/.

of 2020's Q1, Alibaba reported some 846 million mobile monthly active users, "up by 17% year-over-year from 721 million."[346]

Alibaba has historically been light on physical assets with the company's "strategic imperative...to make sure that the platform provided all the resources, or access to the resources, that an online business would need to succeed, and hence supported the evolution of the ecosystem."[347] Given Alibaba's focus on software, it is not surprising that it also owns its own payment method for all of its platforms and beyond. As China and other countries become increasingly cashless—barcode mobile payments reached $3.23 trillion in China in 2018[348]—Alibaba's Alipay has become one of the major cashless players, with some 1.2 billion users as of 2020.[349] As early as 2011, however, Alibaba has made significant investments into the physical side of logistics as well by building a network of warehouses across China.[350]

However, Alibaba, and Alipay in particular, is not without competition. Tencent, the gaming and social media giant with a similar market capitalization of around half a trillion dollars (US audiences might be familiar with Fortnite, the massively popular

---

346 "Alibaba Mobile Monthly Active Users (MAUs)," Marketplace Pulse, accessed October 12, 2020, https://www.marketplacepulse.com/stats/alibaba/alibaba-mobile-monthly-active-users-maus-24#:~:text=Users%20who%20used%20one%20of,over%2Dyear%20from%20721%20million.

347 Ming Zeng, "Alibaba and the Future of Business," *Harvard Business Review* (September-October 2018): 88–96 https://hbr.org/2018/09/alibaba-and-the-future-of-business.

348 "China Is Moving Toward a Cashless Society," *eMarketer,*last modified November 25, 2019, https://www.emarketer.com/content/china-is-moving-toward-a-cashless-society.

349 Emma Lee and Nicole Jao, "Meituan Faces Challenge from Alipay on its Home Turf," *Technode,*last modified April 1, 2020, https://technode.com/2020/04/01/meituan-faces-challenge-from-alipay-on-its-home-turf/.

350 "Alibaba to Spend Billions on Warehouse Network in China," *MH&L*, last modified January 10, 2011, https://www.mhlnews.com/global-supply-chain/article/22038725/alibaba-to-spend-billions-on-warehouse-network-in-china.

game published by Epic Games, "in which Tencent holds a 40% stake"[351]) operates one of China's other super apps, WeChat. As social media sites like Facebook and Instagram are blocked in China, WeChat serves as much more than a messaging platform. Not only can its "monthly user base of more than 1 billion people"[352] post pictures and videos and play games on WeChat, users also have the option of the app's built-in payment service, WeChat Pay. By 2018, Alipay—which had formerly "powered 81% of online payments in China," commanded 54% of the market, with WeChat Pay close behind at 38%.[353] In addition to serving as a form of payment, WeChat, in 2018, also became host to the CPC's rollout of digital ID cards, meant as an "alternative to the physical cards in use."[354] Although it is difficult to make comparisons due to huge cultural differences, in an American context, this would be something like merging one's social security card with one's Facebook Messenger account.

Although many users have sold goods over WeChat, the platform lagged behind Alibaba in the retail sphere without its own designated marketplace. As retail is "40% to 45% of the GDP of China,"[355] Tencent acquired a 20% share in JD.com, the massive e-commerce company. In a partnership that *Reuters* declared going "straight for Alibaba's throat," Tencent's investment was crucial to the profit-low company, which, since its 1998 founding,

351 Adam Lashinsky, "Alibaba v. Tencent."

352 Arjun Kharpal, "Everything You Need to Know about WeChat—China's Billion-User Messaging App," *CNBC*, last modified February 4, 2019, https://www.cnbc.com/2019/02/04/what-is-wechat-china-biggest-messaging-app.html.

353 Adam Lashinsky, "Alibaba v. Tencent."

354 Li Tao, "A Look at China's Push for Digital National ID Cards," *South China Morning Post*, last modified January 23, 2018, https://www.scmp.com/tech/article/2129957/look-chinas-push-national-digital-id-cards.

355 Adam Lashinsky, "Alibaba v. Tencent."

has "concentrated on building up its logistics infrastructure, controlling the supply chain from product purchases to delivery."[356] In addition, WeShop, the integration of WeChat's platform and JD.com's merchandise, looks to take on Taobao and Tmall. With Tencent also ceding "a couple of its e-commerce holdings to JD" in the deal, as well as Walmart selling its "Yihaodian platform to JD in exchange for shares," JD is, as the *Motley Fool* argues, "on a collision course with Alibaba."[357]

If that business model—"[taking] possession of the goods sold on its platform, and [fulfilling] orders with its own warehouses and logistics network"[358]—sounds familiar to you, you're not alone. Recognizing JD's similarities to Amazon has likely prompted some other major investors. In 2016, Walmart acquired a significant stake in the company,[359] and Google sells "JD's products in several overseas markets via Google Shopping."[360] Not only is JD a good investment for those wishing to compete against Alibaba, it's also a pointed investment in a future and seemingly inevitable Amazon-JD showdown.

Alibaba is currently making inroads in US markets, often coming up against other members of the Big 5. In 2019, Alibaba.com

356 Paul Carsten, "Tencent-JD.com Partnership Goes Straight for Alibaba's Throat," *Reuters*, last modified March 9, 2014, https://www.reuters.com/article/us-jd-tencent-hldg/ tencent-jd-com-partnership-goes-straight-for-alibabas-throat-idUSBREA2902T20140310.

357 Billy Duberstein, "JD.com Now Has the Backing of 3 Giant Companies in Its Battle With Alibaba," *The Motley Fool*, last modified June 29, 2018, https://www.fool.com/investing/2018/06/29/jdcom-now-has-the-backing-of-3-giant-companies-in.aspx.

358 Leo Sun, "Where Will JD.com Be in 10 Years?" *The Motley Fool*, last modified July 28, 2019, https:// www.fool.com/investing/2019/07/28/where-will-jdcom-be-in-10-years.aspx.

359 Leo Sun, "Walmart and JD.com Tighten Their Alliance With a $500 Million Investment," *The Motley Fool*, last modified August 12, 2018, https://www.fool.com/investing/2018/08/12/walmart-jdcom-tighten-alliance-500-million-invest.aspx.

360 Ibid.

allowed US businesses to sell on their business-to-business platform. The marketplace has a "global base of more than 10 million buyers across 190 countries," while Amazon Business only offers access to "millions of online buyers in eight countries."[361] In addition, both Alibaba and JD have made significant inroads in Spanish-speaking markets. In 2017, Alibaba "signed a deal with Mexico's state-backed trade and investment group, Promexico, to export products—like avocados and tequila—to China through its e-commerce platform,"[362] and in 2018, JD "opened its Spanish website Joybuy.es for beta testing...to target Spain and Latin America."[363]

Though Alibaba may become a more dominant presence in the West first, JD remains a company to watch. Their control over and ownership of huge parts of their business have allowed them considerable control over the quality and delivery of their merchandise, particularly during the pandemic. As the *Motley Fool* said, "Though JD's heavy investments in logistics, employees, warehouses, and technology have come at a steep price in the past, the long-term strategic benefit of those investments is coming to the fore right now. That's why JD appears poised to take more market share in China's e-commerce industry as China comes out of the COVID-19 slowdown, and likely for the long-term as well."[364]

---

361 Chris Hudgins and Katie Arcieri, "Alibaba, Amazon Battle over US B2B Market with Rival Platforms," *S&P Global*, last modified December 12, 2019, https://www.spglobal.com/marketintelligence/en/news-insights/latest-news-headlines/alibaba-amazon-battle-over-us-b2b-market-with-rival-platforms-55774891.

362 Leo Sun, "Alibaba Is Expanding Its E-Commerce Platform Into These 4 Markets," *The Motley Fool*, last modified September 1, 2018, https://www.fool.com/investing/2018/09/01/alibaba-is-expanding-its-e-commerce-platform-into.aspx.

363 Emma Lee, "JD expands its e-Commerce Empire to Spanish-Speaking Markets," *Technode*, last modified April 17, 2018, https://technode.com/2018/04/17/jd-spanish/.

364 Billy Duberstein, "Amid Coronavirus, JD.com Has an Advantage Over Rivals," *The Motley Fool*, last modified March 23, 2020, https://www.fool.com/investing/2020/03/23/amid-coronavirus-jdcom-has-an-advantage-over-rival.aspx.

As a final note, whenever the Asian e-commerce giants do become better established in the West, it will be with systems and practices more advanced than their American counterparts. Of the well over 100 million parcels delivered every day in China, 70 percent of them are delivered same-day.[365] JD delivers over 90 percent of its orders, either "same-day or next-day by [its] own fleet..."[366] As "more than half of China's 1.3 billion population lives in rural areas," Alibaba and JD's goal of delivery within forty-eight hours to any destination is impressive, to say the least.[367] Realizing these goals has included increased automation and robotics, such as parcel lockers and autonomous ground vehicles that use facial recognition in delivery. In addition, JD has been recruiting "locals who can use their community ties to offer quality service," especially in areas where there "might not be street names or street signage..."[368] We will see how this combination of flexibility, innovation, and seemingly limitless amounts of resources play out in the global marketplace.

365 Juan Sotolongo, Marek Rozycki, and Ian Kerr, "JD vs Alibaba in the Last Mile: What's Happening behind the Great Wall," *Parcel and Postal Technology International*, last modified February 4, 2019, https://www.parcelandpostaltechnologyinternational.com/analysis/jd-vs-alibaba-in-the-last-mile-whats-happening-behind-the-great-wall.html.

366 Ibid.

367 Ibid.

368 Ibid.

CHAPTER 15

ENSURE YOUR BUSINESS SURVIVES AND THRIVES

So, we are now back to where we started. Your idea is great. Your product rocks. Your customers love you. Your team is smart and driven. You've invested tens of thousands, hundreds of thousands, millions of dollars into your business.

Yes, the competitive environment is difficult, but success is possible and well within your grasp. What's next to make sure your business survives and thrives for the next two, five, or ten years?

Here are a few simple places where you can start making gains today:

SHIPPING

1. **Complete the shipping strategy assessment in Appendix B or at jeremybodenhamer.com.** This is an easy first step in analyzing your current processes. It should take no more than ten minutes to complete and will give you an easy-to-understand, simplified evaluation that can be used to develop your plan of attack.

2. **Carrier contract negotiations.** Consider hiring professionals to help in negotiating your carrier agreements. Yes, most firms take a big chunk of the savings they deliver, but these fees are negotiable and typically not fully realizable without sophisticated software that can analyze historical billing files. It will also be a great learning experience to work with industry pros, most of whom are ex-FedEx and ex-UPS employees, to go through a granular approach to rate-building.

3. **Maintain accurate and complete inventory data.** There are plenty of warehouse management systems out there, both lightweight and robust. Buy one! Whatever you choose to use, make sure you maintain accurate and complete data. Real item data is imperative to matching each buyer's unique order with optimal shipping carriers and services, which is imperative if you hope to determine the lowest cost for meeting delivery promises.

4. **Use comprehensive, multi-carrier shipping software.** Use the multi-carrier rating software that is appropriate for your business stage. A $99 per month garbage-in garbage-out approach will increase your per order shipment costs. If you are only shipping fifty orders a week, the savings will be in the software, so an inexpensive product is typically the right move. As your volume increases, shipping overspend will far outweigh the cost of the more expensive software that will take a comprehensive approach to automating carrier and service selection.

5. **Expect more from your shipping API**. Don't skip the ship-spend analysis step if your business uses a shipping API solution. The same rules apply to shipping API vendors that apply to those with interfaces and/or integrations. Compare the providers that are appropriate for your business stage. Have them analyze your ship-spend to see if 1) you are properly/fully utilizing the APIs; and 2) if switching will reduce your costs and provide you with additional controls.

6. **Always use software to manage carrier tariffs.** I hope that

I've persuaded you that carrier contracts are too complex to manage manually. If carrier discounts have been negotiated, the utilization of the tariff and minimums should be managed by software to ensure you realize the negotiated discounts. Make sure you are calculating packed weights and DIMs and rerating before final carrier selection.

7. **Work with solutions that scale.** Make sure all software vendors are capable of scaling with your business before you purchase, unless you want to re-platform frequently, which is expensive and time-consuming. Work with solutions that support dynamic or low-lift workflow customizations/updates to support the inevitable changes in inventory types and customer buying behaviors. Use rule-based software so that orders receive proper treatment from customer, cost, and service perspectives.

8. **Stop promising customers carrier services by name.** It only helps the carrier when you name your shipping services by their names (i.e., FedEx, UPS, USPS, etc.). Stop it! Don't promise customers specific carriers; promise delivery times. Most customers don't care about the color of the truck that pulls up to the house. They care about when their order is scheduled to arrive. Align your promises to those needs. Use one-day, two-day, ground, and express labels and leave out specific carrier names. This gives you the leeway to meet the delivery promise at the lowest possible cost.

9. **Analyze returns processes.** Remember that "replacing a damaged product can cost an e-commerce vendor up to seventeen times more than the original cost to ship."[369] Do all items need to be returned? Does it make sense to partner with returns

---

369 Kyla Fisher and Bob Lilianfeld, "Optimizing Packaging for an E-commerce World," Ameripen: American Institute for Packaging and the Environment, last modified January, 2017, https://cdn.ymaws.com/www.ameripen.org/resource/resmgr/PDFs/White-Paper-Optimizing-Packa.pdf.

providers like Happy Returns or Returnly? Take returns seriously, and don't treat them as uncontrollable.

PACKING

1. **Optimize order fulfillment workflows.** Don't assume your workflow is the right workflow just because it's always been done that way. Analyze automation components, picking accuracy and speed, carton and packaging selection, packing efficiency, order composition, ship-from locations, back order processes, mispicks, damage, and every other component of your workflow. As you can see in The Black Tux Case Study in Appendix A, workflows can be complex. It pays to look at your processes with fresh eyes.

2. **Use environmentally friendly, biodegradable packaging whenever possible.** Don't just use it; make sure your customers know that you are making environmentally friendly choices. Remind them that more than one billion trees are cut down each year for US shipment packaging, and you are helping to change that.[370]

3. **If you have enough volume, invest in box-making hardware.** The minimums to justify the expense are not small, but the variable pricing model is a great way to allow smaller shippers access to custom box-making hardware that is environmentally friendly and delivers a great ROI. Many of these machines are now API compatible, which means your cartonization logic can tell the machine the exact specs of each carton without manual measuring or using data entry. To access the variable pricing model, you frequently have to agree to buy the cardboard from the machine retailer.

---

370 Jon Bird, "What A Waste: Online Retail's Big Packaging Problem," *Forbes*, last modified July 29, 2018, https://www.forbes.com/sites/jonbird1/2018/07/29/what-a-waste-online-retails-big-packaging-problem/#4ad1dad6371d.

4. **Use bin packing solutions.** Use smart packing software to minimize carton sizes, carrier DIM weight charges, and unnecessary shipments of air. Don't let this good deed go unnoticed. Tell your customers that you are making earth-friendly choices and not contributing to the excess "24 million of the 60 million truckloads of product shipped annually in the United States," which are the result of shipping boxes that are too big. Remember, you are contributing to "sav[ing] 1.75 billion gallons of diesel [and] preventing 17 billion kilograms of carbon dioxide from entering the atmosphere."[371]

WAREHOUSING

1. **Fully utilize your first DC before expanding.** Every square inch, wall to wall, and floor to ceiling. Upgrade your racks, add mezzanine levels, and investigate goods-to-person inventory robotics whenever appropriate. Only then should additional facilities be considered. Yes, speed of service and shipping costs are ongoing concerns. Even if you elect to open an additional DC, the aim should be to have full utilization of the entire cube.

2. **Ship from as many locations as is cost-effective.** Yes, it is not necessarily realistic for small sellers or those not wanting to carry excess inventories or safety stock. Shipping from more than one location does increase inventory costs. Although depending on where those distribution points are located, it also has the power to significantly decrease ship costs and delivery times. Include inventory cost adjustments in your analysis prior to expanding. Remember, the research shows

371 Gary Forger, "Sustainable Packaging Is Ready to Make ts Mark," *Logistics Management*, Online, last modified September 1, 2019, https://www.logisticsmgmt.com/article/ sustainable_packaging_is_ready_to_make_its_mark.

that with two strategically placed DCs, companies can reach 90 percent of the US via ground shipping in two days.[372]

3. **Research dynamic warehousing offerings.** Dynamic warehousing companies offer an easy way to dip your toe in the water. They don't normally require long-term commitments and will let you occupy as little as a single pallet space. Companies like Flowspace, STORD, and Flexe have built nationwide networks of dynamic warehouses and cross-docks to bring down costs and allow shippers to easily reposition products. These providers can also help with seasonal scale.

4. **Look into 3PLs with offerings built for your stage.** Just like matching shipping software products for your business stage, you also must match third-party logistics (3PL) fulfillment options. Shopify and Shipwire are good examples of fulfillment networks built for small businesses. They will store, pick, pack, and ship your products so you can focus on selling. Just remember, many 3PLs mark up shipping rates so using a 3PL does not remove the necessity for you to do your own independent carrier negotiations alongside your 3PL discussions. Doing so will give you a full understanding of all your options and the associated costs.

5. **Standardize performance standards across all channels.** The highest margin channels should meet or beat the delivery experience on lower margin channels. If a marketplace is taking a big cut of the pie, and you want customers to buy directly from your website, make sure you deliver the order at least as well as the marketplace. This doesn't just mean fast; this also means keeping the customer up to date on the status of their order. In fact, you may be able to enhance the delivery experience enough through status updates that your customer

---

372 "COVID-19: Shipping & Fulfillment Continuity Action Plan," ShipHawk, last modified March 2020, https://info.shiphawk.com/covid-19-shipping-and-fulfillment-continuity-action-plan-social.

would still rate your delivery higher if the shipment took a day longer to reach their doorstep. Buyers love order updates!

DATA AND ANALYTICS

1. **Own your data.** This is imperative. Do not use free software provided by a shipping carrier or nonneutral supplier who uses that data internally to determine pricing policies. In the end, this will cost you. The free component is a sales tactic to get you to move more volume to assets they control. I have yet to see one of these systems that is truly multi-carrier, even though they are sold as such. True rate optimization is not possible under these circumstances as the provider will always be looking for ways to insert their products, thereby systematically misrouting shipments to less than optimal carriers and services.

2. **Track real shipping costs and losses.** Even if you book shipping cost as a marketing budget line-item, track CAC (customer acquisition cost) separately. Merge the two later if you must but know each number independently. Why? Because free shipping converts, it doesn't acquire new customers. Knowing your distribution costs on an order-by-order and customer-by-customer basis will help you determine if your pricing, promotions, and target customers are appropriate and profitable.

3. **Improve customer communication.** As the vast majority of consumers (85 percent) expect to be able to monitor their orders every step of the way, keeping customers updated throughout the entire order lifecycle becomes increasingly important. Post-purchase software can give customers the control to update shipments, access replacement inventory, and process their own returns. Some WMSs "even provide customers with automatic order updates so they can stay

informed as [the shipper] prepare[s] their order for delivery."[373]
Overcommunicate! Here are a few minimum communication
points:

- Has the order been received?
- Is it being picked/processed?
- Has the label been printed?
- Has the carrier picked it up?
- Is it scheduled for delivery today?
- Has the return been received?
- Has a credit been issued?

4. **Review the baseline operational metrics.** A business would
   never allow a sales leader to run a sales org without specific
   sales metrics like weighted pipeline, average contract value,
   and sales cycle. So why are operations leaders running warehouse operations without a set of standard metrics and
   targets? Step one is to measure. Step two is to create targets
   and manage your teams to your chosen targets. I've listed some
   baseline operations metrics in Appendix C to get you started.

5. **Consider creating a digital twin.** For operations with the
   resources, consider feeding all of your warehouse data into
   one system and creating a digital twin to simulate warehouse
   operations and permutations. This will help ensure you are
   making data-driven decisions. A digital twin should definitely
   be considered prior to building a new warehouse or completing
   a redesign.

---

373 "Improve Customer Service with Warehouse Management Software," Scanco, published
    December 18, 2018, http://web.archive.org/web/20171122005836/http://www.scanco.com/
    improve-customer-service-with-warehouse-management-software/.

ROBOTS AND ROBOTICS

If you are not a large shipper, robots are most likely unnecessary. That being said, my sales team speaks with very large shippers on a regular basis who are still using legacy software and manual processes. If this is you, run, don't walk, to your nearest robot superstore and load up. For everyone else:

1. **Use traditional hardware whenever possible.** Traditional hardware like scales, scanners, dimensioners, and conveyors significantly improve efficiencies and worker safety. They help move goods throughout the warehouse, reduce the number of pack stations needed for weighing and measuring, and reduce or eliminate manual keying of data. These hardware devices provide great advantages for a relatively low cost.

2. **Use scanning functionality.** Scanners are amazing and have underappreciated value. For example, scanners are one of the best weapons in your fight to decrease returns. By using a scan verify process to ensure the right items and only the right items are packed in each box prior to shipping, you reduce your mis-ship items and resulting product returns. Boxes, pick tickets, and shipping labels can all be scanned and managed through appropriate shipping software.

3. **If you aren't labor constrained, consider moving robots to the end of your to-do list.** The order of events is always important, and I'd be remiss if I didn't suggest moving robots down your list and mastering the other suggested categories first. While you do this, costs will continue to drop. Of course, for those who are labor-constrained, this is not an option. The warehouse remains a human-intensive domain. Remove the people, and it stops working. In the face of labor insecurity, robotics must be prioritized.

OPERATIONS WORKERS—THE HUMAN COMPONENT

When I started ShipHawk, I wrote a blog post titled "We Believe." In it, I wrote, "The world is evolving. Main Street is now nothing more than a tourist attraction thanks to the Walmart and Target sitting just outside town and the often-overused Amazon or Alibaba bookmark in your browser. Local, family-owned businesses have been replaced by jobs in massive regional warehouses, where the human is the last great inefficiency and is being rapidly replaced by robots."

The goal isn't to avoid robots. The goal is to invest in people. It's the people who make your business work. It's the people who invent, improve, and create. As we've seen, those people do come at a high cost, but there is also a high cost for not caring for the individuals. Remember that, according to the Gallup survey referenced earlier, almost 20 percent of your workforce is actively disengaged and half of them are "doing just enough work to get by."[374]

With this level of disengagement coupled with the high replacement costs we've discussed, it's not that you can't afford to take care of your people, it's that you can't afford *not* to take care of them.

Keep workers engaged, invest in training, work to reduce turnover, invest in the warehouse environment like you invest in the office environment. Make your working environment part of your brand identity. Take pride in your people, and they will take pride in your business and the work they do for you, creating more value in the process.

---

374 Lisa Harrington, "Warehouse Labor Performance: And the Winner Is...Everyone," Inbound Logistics, last modified May 1, 2008, https://www.inboundlogistics.com/cms/article/warehouse-labor-performance-and-the-winner-iseveryone/.

1. **The first place to start is with your team.** They know your current systems and reasons behind them better than anyone. For example: Have you streamlined multi-online storefront, retail, marketplace, and drop-ship order management? Are you using software to select the right carrier and service for every order? Are you using software to select the optimal distribution point for every order? There are questions for executives, operations, and IT. I've detailed some questions in Appendix D for CEOs and/or company executives to ask their teams in order to determine opportunities for improvement.

2. **Current warehouse conditions leave plenty of room for improvement.** Reevaluate break areas, outdoor spaces, windows (whenever possible), temperature, and sound. I have a friend who runs a large multi-warehouse operation who is taking this seriously and treating his warehouse common areas like he does his office common areas, installing pool tables, ping-pong tables, upgrading coffee machines, artwork, and music for ambiance. By investing in the workers and the environment in which they work, he hopes to reduce turnover and the high costs that come along with it.

3. **Invest in training programs to upskill workers for future assignments.** Operations workers see the business through a different lens and can bring a diversity of perspective to other areas of the business. Invest in training and provide all employees with clear career paths. Giving people a direct line of sight to a better role with more responsibility and higher compensation has the potential to change their perspective of the work they are doing today. Remember, almost 20 percent of your workforce is already disengaged, and half of them are doing just enough to get by. This attitude is costing your business real money. This is an opportunity to put that money to better use.

4. **Stop looking at warehouse team members as disposable.** Change your perspective on the projected tenure of these

employees. High turnover comes at a cost that is not insignificant—about 25 percent of each worker's salary—as we discussed.[375] Invest in these workers and their work environment like you do for those in the front office. Make these improvements part of your DNA so you begin to attract the type of workers who want to engage and invest for the long haul. Remember, nobody in front of the buy button ever made a dollar without the operations team executing behind it.

5. **Consider the benefits of higher wages and benefits.** Hardware, software, and robotics automation will not only reduce operations costs, but will also reduce the number of workers required. Take these savings and invest them back into your workforce and watch productivity and profitability rise.

BUT WAIT, THERE'S MORE

- **Tag stories of your heroic operations workers with #heroclass and #behindthebuybutton.** COVID-19 showed us that the people behind the buy button have historically been invisible. We have taken this hero class for granted. It is time to share their stories and get the word out about all they do for us. Let's celebrate these critical members of our teams!

- Send an email to mailto:info@jeremybodenhamer.com to schedule a time to complete a free Order Fulfillment Efficiency Review—a member of our team will walk you through each component, leaving you with a comprehensive plan of attack.

- You can also visit jeremybodenhamer.com to complete a free Shipping Strategy Assessment or complete the assessment in Appendix B.

---

375 Veronica Donchez, "Warehouse Labor: The 'Real' Cost of Warehouse Worker Turnover," *Kane Logistics*, last modified May 21, 2019, https://www.kaneisable.com/blog/warehouse-labor-the-real-cost-of-warehouse-worker-turnover.

ONE MORE THING...

Some final advice to the independent merchants fighting to win against the giants: be you! Make sure what makes you unique is evident in your business model, messaging, and purpose. People love you and will support you once they know you are authentic. Authenticity, honesty, and data-backed truth have never been more important or more valued in the world. The successful companies of tomorrow will all have made this a core tenant of their mission, values, and messaging.

A section titled, "Authenticity Is Paramount," in the Deloitte study referenced in the predictions above, suggests the true path to success must include:

- **"Tell your story and make it impactful.** Authenticity is rooted in a brand's commitment to creating an impact and sharing its story."
- **"Walk the walk.** Authentic purpose-driven businesses 'walk the walk' by being transparent and accountable for everything they do."
- **"Put all humans at the heart of your decisions.** Brands leading with purpose often occupy a meaningful place in the hearts and minds of *all* the people they touch."
- **"Let purpose evolve with the organization and bond its people.** Every business is founded with a core purpose, but purpose can require nurturing and revisiting too. Stoke your purpose over time, revisit your core DNA, and evolve it inclusively with all your people."[376]

I'd also add one more.

---

376 Diana O'Brien, Andy Main, Suzanne Kounkel, and Anthony R. Stephan, "Purpose Is Everything," *Deloitte*, last modified October 15, 2019, https://www2.deloitte.com/us/en/insights/topics/marketing-and-sales-operations/global-marketing-trends/2020/purpose-driven-companies.html.

- Treat all workers with respect and dignity. The workplace should be great for all classes of employees. Reduce turnover and use that money to improve worker pay, invest in training, and publicize the heck out of those efforts. The world needs you as an example.

These five steps make the environment better for us all. We need more businesses like Parker Clay in the world. Read about them in Appendix A!

APPENDIX A

CASE STUDIES

CASE STUDY: VERISHOP

When Imran Khan, Snapchat's former CSO, and his wife Cate, formerly of Quidsi, were thinking about getting into e-commerce, they began by looking at what the field's three largest marketplaces—Amazon, eBay, and Alibaba—didn't do well. For the couple and their eventual team, this boiled down to three things: authenticity, the shopping experience, and new-brand exposure. "You can get an NFL jersey on Alibaba for twenty-five bucks," said Christopher Cartelli, a founding member of what would become Verishop, as well as its VP of operations, "but you have no way of knowing if it's authenticated on those three sites."

Especially in the luxury realm, counterfeiting is a constant challenge, as counterfeiters have been known to even produce their wares out of the same factories as the brands being replicated. Partially due to their sheer size, e-commerce's "Big

Three" have been notoriously bad at vetting their sellers' items' authenticity, which also contributes to the quality of the overall online shopping experience on their sites. "There's no joy in shopping on those websites," Cartelli said. It's a rather perfunctory process, with no aspect of "finding" a new, treasured item. Creating a platform that could help "people discover new brands, that's a big niche."

Enter Verishop, the online marketplace launched in May of 2019, meticulously designed to address those flaws. Through its "security process and logistics processes," said Cartelli, Verishop is able to guarantee all of its merchandise's authenticity. All of Verishop's offerings go "direct from manufacturing right to us, so [customers] don't have to worry about counterfeiters." With a proprietary system such that every single object is imprinted with something like a "digital fingerprint," Cartelli is also able to ensure that all returned merchandise is also the real deal.

The company's emphasis on customer service—customers are able to reach US-based representatives 24/7, as well as free same and next-day shipping and free returns (the COVID-19 pandemic slowed the company down to two-day shipping)— has resulted in an NPS (Net Promoter Score, which measures consumer experience and loyalty) "in the nineties, which is unheard of in e-commerce," said Cartelli. Finally, Verishop's buyers are looking for all the "up-and-coming brands—we want to make sure we're trying to [source] those," thereby linking customers to suitable products about which they may not have previously known. With its three in-house brands— Ghost Democracy (clean skincare), Billie the Label (high-end women's clothing), and LETT (luxe leisurewear)—Verishop is able to not just build its platform but participate on it as well.

Even considering the sizable startup money that went into Verishop's founding (by November of 2019, they had raised over $30 million[377]), opening a company with all of these sales points fully operable on day one is no easy feat. Not only does Verishop offer free same- or next-day shipping, the company will "hopefully by the end of Q2 get same-day delivery in the major cities." Currently, Verishop's fulfillment is run through a combination of the company's own warehouses in some key locations, as well as contracting with 3PLs in others. In addition, Verishop plans to have an international arm by Q1 of next year, working "with a 3PL solution internationally, [who will] pick up packages, do all the customs, with two- to four-day delivery."

Clearly, Verishop was designed with a shrewd understanding of the e-commerce landscape, as well as with scalability in mind. As Cartelli said, "If you don't get to next-day delivery in the next couple of years, people aren't going to shop on your site." Although the "freeness" of shipping is baked into the merchandise price, "if you don't give this impression that it's free, you're not going to make it out there in the e-commerce world...If you can do same-day for free in the major cities, that's the ticket."

While Verishop is clearly orienting itself toward this future, it is using a mixture of cutting-edge and what might be considered "throwback" approaches to getting there. Cartelli advocates for a strategic blend of partnerships—"never put all your eggs in one basket." In terms of getting something like same-day delivery off the ground, this means a combination of local expertise—"a small to medium [carrier] in a local market"—

377 "Verishop," Crunchbase, accessed October 12, 2020, https://www.crunchbase.com/organization/verishop#section-funding-rounds.

along with a national or international, as the case may be, player. "You have to know your markets," Cartelli said. "In [New York City, for example], a mom-and-pop can do so much better than a FedEx or UPS." All of these contracts should be the result of an "open-book negotiation," whereby both parties benefit—if a local shipper is going out with "80 percent-full, 90 percent-full vans, let me fill that last 10 percent, let me fix that for you [while I] scale. And if you scale really quickly, send the rest to the national player." Such negotiations with carriers can be a neglected aspect of automation processes, but it's one that has helped Verishop become a significant e-commerce presence in such a short time.

From pots made of repurposed ceramic to goods designed, manufactured, and distributed within the US, Verishop has been equally savvy in curating its brands around current consumer trends. Yet, as with any successful marketplace—digital or otherwise—the company's strength is not in its vendors nearly as much as in its platform. The inherent scalability of this business model, along with its own efforts to remain immune to counterfeiting—the company's intense focus on customer service makes it difficult to be imitated by an Amazon or eBay, for instance—seed Verishop with enormous growth potential. Just as some of Verishop's approaches to future-oriented market success aren't necessarily "tech-forward," its presence also reestablishes something quickly disappearing from big e-commerce: healthy competition.

CASE STUDY: PARKER CLAY

As we saw with Verishop, one method of establishing independence from the giant e-commerce retailers is by tailoring one's business to fill in niche areas and markets ignored or underserved elsewhere. Another method, however, can be found in reconsidering how business itself is done.

For Parker Clay, the Santa Barbara and Addis Ababa Ethiopia-based leather goods company, "business as usual" in the traditional retail, or even e-commerce sense does not exist. Created and built with a sense of impact in mind that many other companies don't consider, Parker Clay, says co-founder and CEO, Ian Bentley, is "not just the creation of a job—it's almost like potentially changing the next generation of the country." Parker Clay employs 140 people in its Ethiopia factory, 80 percent of whom are women, and many of whom have experienced prostitution or trafficking of some kind. Having seen an aid model to both stimulate development and interrupt the cycle of poverty being used in Ethiopia, Bentley and his wife thought to try the "trade" method instead, whereby vulnerable women were given gainful employment, and thereby independently empowered.

As Bentley said, the "fashion industry has been a black box forever, and that's been by design, where brands historically sought to limit the customer's understanding of the way their business works in order to really control the narrative." But, as today's consumer is "far more of an activist than they've ever been before, there is mounting pressure for fashion brands to show the depth of the claims they're making [about] transparency and sustainability." In stark contrast to this, Parker Clay's main selling point, besides the objects themselves, is precisely in how and why these objects are made.

Part of fashion's "black box" is its obfuscation of its supply chain. There are a whole host of intermediary steps between the garment and the consumer. Without even considering the raw materials' sourcing, traditional retail begins in a factory, whose goods then encounter a brand's sales representatives, followed by wholesale processes and additional movement and warehousing before eventually reaching the consumer. It is, to put it mildly, a sector with many "touches." According to Bentley, all of these "touches" are moments in which companies can lose control and oversight of their products, making claims of transparency or sustainability difficult to make, much less believe.

One of Parker Clay's main business innovations is a return to prior forms of manufacturing, in that they own or are directly involved with every aspect of its supply chain. Not only does the company own its factory in Ethiopia, it actively sources the leather from which its goods are made. Ethiopia, said Bentley, "has the fifth largest population of livestock in the world, and it also has a really ancient tanning industry...There's a sought-after premium to the product that I discovered when we were living there, and I bought this bag for my wife that I randomly found in a market and it says, 'Made in Ethiopia' inside." Stunned by the quality of the leather, Bentley began doing research. "I went to a tannery and talked to the owner. The day that I went there, he happened to be loading a huge forty-foot shipping container with leather, and I asked him, 'Where are you taking this?' and he [said], 'I'm shipping this off to Italy.'" That, for Bentley, was an aha moment, in which he better understood not just the stops in the fashion industry's supply chain, but also the incredible quality of Ethiopian leather.

Working directly with local communities, Parker Clay has tapped into this resource. "Ninety percent of Ethiopia is living off the land—they're farmers," said Bentley, with animals helping "provide for families...At the end of its life, the [animal's] hides might be discarded, so in a way, it's almost like this byproduct that people are like 'What will we do with this'— because there is a leather industry, it's allowed these farmers... to sell this byproduct and make additional revenue, and it allows us to turn that into a product that could have normally been discarded as waste." So, though some might view leather itself as an inherently unsustainable material, Parker Clay views it as "a very impact-oriented component, where it could have been [discarded], and it's creating economic opportunity for those families and small farmers. And we're able to turn it into a beautiful product that we back with a lifetime guarantee."

Once the products have been manufactured in Ethiopia, they are shipped to Parker Clay's distribution center in Santa Barbara, from which they are sent out either directly to the consumer or to the company's retail site. In other words, aside from its time in transit, Parker Clay has full control over its merchandise at every point, from the sourcing of raw materials, to manufacturing, to distribution. As the fulfillment center used to be Bentley's garage, everything remains close to home: "We receive all of our shipments from Ethiopia, inspect them, and go through the process to get them prepared for filling orders. And then we are shipping pretty much Monday through Friday. During peak seasons, we ship in reality seven days a week."

With some exceptions for big order spikes, Parker Clay fulfills all orders within twenty-four hours, and, in some cases, the same day. "If it's Mother's Day on Sunday, we'll get it out same-day on Friday, or if there's another kind of key event, we make sure to get it out same-day," said Bentley. "That's what our website advertises, and we stick to it." This commitment to, as well as the nature of its claims has inspired a customer base that doesn't just trust the company but associates its goods with a distinct narrative: "In Santa Barbara, we had these mud-slides here a few years ago...There was a woman who lost a few of her children in that, and she was in the hospital. She came into our shop right after she got out...and she walked in, and she said 'I had such an amazing community around me that supported me and loved me through this that I just couldn't think of a better gift to give them.'"

Working to restore the "discontinuity between producer to consumer" has helped Parker Clay tap into and expand upon ideas of community, as well as demonstrate how a company can successfully commodify a more considered way of doing business. This level of consideration extends even to Parker Clay's metrics. While "most e-commerce businesses have 25-30 percent returning customers,"[378] Parker Clay's "range between 30 to 40%." As for returns—which have long plagued e-commerce with rates up to quadruple its brick-and-mortar equivalent—Parker Clay averages 5.9 percent, versus an industry high of 40 percent.[379] Though these numbers are significant in demonstrating Parker Clay's relationship with its consumers, they also have more far-reaching implications.

378 "Percent Returning Customers," *Geckoboard*, accessed October 12, 2020, https://www.geckoboard.com/best-practice/kpi-examples/percent-returning-customers/.

379 Courtney Reagan, "That Sweater You Don't Like Is a Trillion-Dollar Problem for Retailers. These Companies Want to Fix It," *CNBC*, last modified January 12, 2020, https://www.cnbc.com/2019/01/10/growing-online-sales-means-more-returns-and-trash-for-landfills.html.

As analysts have pointed out, repeat customers are one of a business' most profitable assets: not only does a third-time customer have double the likelihood of purchasing a product as a first-time customer, a repeat customer visiting a website has a 60 to 70 percent chance of converting to a sale, versus the average conversion rate of 1 to 3 percent.[380]

Thus Parker Clay has shown that ethical treatment of its workers—as well as a respect for the value of the labor they provide and the impacts this labor can have—is an innovation in itself that has made them both competitive and impactful.

---

380 Alex McEachern, "What is a Repeat Customer and Why are they Profitable?" *smile.io*, last modified February, 2020, https://blog.smile.io/repeat-customers-profitable/.

CASE STUDY: THE BLACK TUX

In 2012, Mike Gammarino was the newly minted co-founder and VP of operations for Santa Monica, California-based The Black Tux, a startup with a fast-growing business that was dependent on slow-moving SMB shipping software.

So, Mike set to work, and in a short amount of time, built a warehouse automation system so effective that he now designs and deploys similar systems full-time in his role as founder and president of Bluprint Partners where, according to the company website, he helps "e-commerce operators exceed the demands of explosive growth." From new warehouses to shipping and inventory infrastructures, and complex post-purchase products services, Mike helps companies grow fast without crashing.

One of The Black Tux co-founders had a wedding," Gammarino said, "and if you look at his wedding pictures, I mean the guys were *swimming* in their tuxes. There's got to be another way! [But] there really wasn't any other option." So, Mike and his partners built one, from the ground up.

Seeing a white space in the market, Gammarino and what would become The Black Tux's other co-founders went and tried on suits from many different vendors and found that the "modern man" didn't have a suitable rental option that offered appealing cuts or fits. Starting from scratch, they sourced their own suit and tux patterns, against the existing "old baggy styles from the 90s." Their commitment to modernizing tux rental required complex supply chain processes. From garment design to in-house tailor and cobbler services, all aspects of production and fulfillment had to be rethought under this new aesthetic.

"When we started, we didn't know if it was a good idea to out-source [order fulfillment] or if we should in-house it and do it ourselves because there is some uniqueness about the rental business that actually makes it not optimal to send it to some-body else. Typically, third-party logistics and warehouses want a fairly simple standard order picking and packing process. However, when you're dealing with more unique products... it's better to keep it in-house." Not only were the objects and their packaging nonstandard—garments shipped and stored on hangers, along with shoes, belts, ties, etc.—100 percent of sales were returned. "Warehouse 3PLs hate returns," Gam-marino said, "and we also provided hemming services to the jackets and the pants. In addition to the fact that we had to dry clean returns, we actually built an internal dry-cleaning facility inside of our warehouse."

All of that was housed in The Black Tux's first location, which, at 1,000 square feet, also included their office and a small retail space. Within six months, The Black Tux had so outgrown their space that they moved into a 12,000 square-foot DC. A year and a half later, they moved again, this time to a 50,000 square-foot warehouse. Within two years, the company had grown spatially some fifty times over.

At the 50,000 square-foot mark, they began thinking, "We need to look at putting some automation in." So, they did. "We upgraded our warehouse management system to a tier 1 for the facility—HighJump, which is kind of top of the heap." Used by companies such as Canada Dry, Peet's, and 99 Cents Only, HighJump wasn't the obvious choice for the still relatively small The Black Tux. "We were probably one of the smallest warehouses that they had ever done a HighJump install for. We knew that going in, but we also knew that we were growing fast, and eventually, we would expand to the East Coast—and we have a facility in Pennsylvania now, too. We wanted to make sure our systems [were] good [for scaling] and could also be copied to another location in the country."

At that original 50,000 square-foot warehouse, "we put in moving conveyors, we put RFID tags inside of every garment so that when product came back for the return—if you have six or seven products inside of a box—shoes, shirt, tie, belt, pants, jacket—all those items will be scanned in one pass, and they would immediately be checked back into our system and then they would work their way through the sorting and the dry-cleaning process. We built an automated returns processor that would bring the boxes in, open them, and then we had people sort [the] different items. And then on the outbound, we had an automated conveyor that we would use to help the operators make their picking more efficient. [The operators] wore a kind of digital read-out on their wrist that would tell them what to pick, [and] they would put it on the automated conveyor. It would carry the garment toward the front where they would be joined up...so, you put a jacket, and then the pants would come and be married with it, you'd have the shoes—as they came, the system would tell you where to put it and where it was from. And then we had a conveyor system that pushed the orders out, [and] got scanned by the RFID scanner on the way out, just to make sure that if there were supposed to be six items in the box, there were actually six items in the box, and they were the correct items, and then an automatic label would be slapped on, and it would go out the door."

According to Gammarino, the benefits from these implementations were enormous. "We probably increased our efficiency in that facility close to 40 to 50 percent. Meaning the staff could produce about twice as many orders out the door as they could before. Reduction in time, reduction in errors, and then increase in just efficiency of the way that they worked."

The Black Tux also used automation to help streamline the consumer-facing side of the business. As they were dealing with an extremely variable product—"if we had a guy that's 6'7", we don't have a pair of pants that fits that guy, unless you take the hem out"—accurate and predictive sizing became a valuable tool. Not just height, Gammarino says, but also age became an important metric in gauging fit: "A guy that is six-feet tall and 21 has a different body type than the man at 65. In fact, they even wear their pants in a different location... if you know old movies from the fifties and sixties, men wear their pants really high, by their belly button...so, we would take that into consideration because they would actually need a bit of a longer pant that was higher on the waist, and then your body type changes over time. We took all that into account and used machine learning to essentially try to predict what [customers'] measurements would be in terms of our coats, our jackets, and our pants." With the help of almost three years' worth of data and a statistician, The Black Tux built a predictive tool that has continued to help them further improve the very thing that got them into business—the perfect fit.

CASE STUDY: GROVE COLLABORATIVE

In the last eight years, Grove has gone from three friends haul-ing orders to their local post office in San Francisco to three fulfillment centers around the US with 1,500 employees and counting. "Grove was created with the vision of making con-sumer products a positive force and specifically with a mission around helping families find products that reflect the best for themselves and their homes," said Stuart Landesberg, Grove's co-founder and CEO.

Part of Grove's explosive growth has to do with its "direct rela-tionship with the consumer," which has enabled the company to figure out and offer the products people actually want. As today's more environmentally conscious consumers transition from the products of their childhood, Grove is there to help them make educated decisions that are "safer for them and better for the planet." That means not only a carefully curated selection of third-party brands chosen for ingredients as well as the business practices of the companies behind them, but also five in-house brands. From tree-free paper products offered under Seedling by Grove to 100 percent recycled plas-tic trash bags by Grove Collaborative to Roven, a "new beauty retail concept" that offers all things clean beauty, Grove is becoming both the marketplace and one of the key purveyors of clean-living products.

Along with consumer-facing aspects like customer service, Landesberg attributes Grove's relationship with its consumer to his and his team's keen eye for and use of data. Grove Guide—a "hybrid between a personal shopper and customer support"—interacts with up to 10,000 customers a week, which produces "hundreds of thousands of data points around which products are resonating with customers, which aren't, what is being done well, and what people are excited about." Collecting and analyzing this data gives the company strong insights into the market and its customers. When this user data is combined with sales data and information generated by Grove's active social media community, there results "alchemy in terms of product development."

However, Landesberg is quick to point out, data requires inter-pretation to make it meaningful: "the existence of data does not necessarily mean accurate insight, and so while we've always had a really data-driven company, I've also really been surprised and impressed to [the degree that] human intuition was really necessary to make sure that people understand the story that the data is [telling]." For Grove, data may be valu-able, "but the insights that come from it are largely relying on a strong team over anything else. You can tell I'm very much a team-is-the-only-thing-that-matters person."

This belief in the importance of the role of human understand-ing and team insights has carried over into Grove's fulfillment centers. "I think humans with good data and good planning are much more likely to be successful than automation," Landes-berg said. As the company was originally growing, Grove looked into an expansive automation installation in a fulfillment center, a "seven-figure thing." They "calculated the payback, and spent all this time on it, [but] it never actually ended up happening." In the intervening months, however, by "improving the team, improving practices, improving protocol—we did end up getting all those efficiency gains without ever actually doing the project."

Such improvements for Grove involve utilizing a data insight to streamline the fulfillment process: "a good system to understand is how wide a pick-face should be based on how much volume a SKU is doing." By using data to track a relatively simple metric like units per day, per item, the length of the pick-pass was drastically reduced, which led to an improvement in efficiency "as large as potentially some really big, crazy software automation."

Another relatively simple data point that Grove works with is the fact that 80 percent of its customers also have Amazon Prime, but, said Landesberg, consumers "trust Grove in a different way than the other marketplaces." By offering "quality, sustainability, health, [and] the ability to feel comfortable [and] good about your home and your family," along with the products themselves, Grove's entire consumer dynamic presents itself as a "powerful differentiator from pretty much everyone on the market."

This sense of trust and comfort is not easily replicable, especially by e-commerce giants who have shown themselves to be less concerned with issues of sustainability and environmental impact in particular. In building such a platform, Grove has been able to be the sole purveyor of its in-house brands and offers subscription and bulk options for frequently purchased items. In the end, it seems that Landesberg's mantra for how to run a business is just as applicable to Grove's ethos as a whole: "the best results come from simpler systems and well-organized people."

CASE STUDY: FLOYD HOME

By now, it's faster to name the industries that have not been fundamentally changed by e-commerce than to list those that have. Back in 2014, the founders of Floyd—a home furnishings designer and retailer based in Detroit, Michigan—saw what was even then a rare opportunity: bringing e-commerce to the furniture market. "Our core customer," said Aaron Turk, VP of operations and corporate development at Floyd, "is the young professional that's living in an urban environment, generally in smaller-space apartments [who is] seeking to have something higher quality from a brand that resonates with them." In addition, this customer, primarily of the millennial generation, is extremely "tech-savvy, [and has been] trained to buy everything else online. Furniture is one of those last [areas]," said Turk. So much so that nearly 90 percent of Floyd's sales come through e-commerce. "We have several strategic partnerships across other channels like retail and office," said Turk, "with West Elm as the most prominent. Each channel helps to drive incremental sales and increase the awareness of our brand.

That brand is precisely what separates Floyd from its competitors. As opposed to other e-commerce furniture purveyors—think Wayfair, and, of course, Amazon—Floyd envisioned itself as a company with a sustainable message and mission. Floyd was founded as a reaction to the disposable furniture trend. Its furniture is made to last, modular for ease of moving, sustainably sourced, and responsibly manufactured entirely in the US. Floyd's competitive advantage, said Turk, "...starts with the product design but flows through the entire supply chain."

Knowing that they didn't want to compete on price, selection, or speed with the e-commerce giants, Floyd instead has focused on the quality and design of its products, which stems from its relationship with and knowledge of its customer. "We want to create the best product possible," said Turk. To this end, Floyd only makes a comparatively few products, but it designs them to fully fit its brand, which means intuitive, durable, sustainable, and desirable. "We're able to offer a premium product at an accessible price point that can be delivered in a very reasonable time," he continued. By surveying its customers, Floyd found that an extremely fast shipping time wasn't as important as other factors like in-home delivery, and the ability to schedule times. With that in mind, the company has partnered with various outfits that help it prioritize its customers' specific shipping and delivery needs. One example is Convey, a delivery experience management platform, which, said Turk, "enables visibility and transparency into our last mile delivery network, which helps us provide a better customer experience." The team at Floyd even pulled Convey's shipping data and predictions into its CRM tool, Kustomer, to automate and streamline customer issue resolution to reduce cost-to-serve while making customers even happier.

Floyd was designed to be an e-commerce disruptor, not just in terms of its consumer-facing practices, but so too on its backend. Part of the company's sustainability mission plays out in warehouse optimization, which is no small feat when considering furniture. "We design all of our products as a kit of parts that can be flat-packed, which allows us to minimize transportation and warehousing costs, and maintain a lean inventory model. We have a network of domestic manufacturers located in the Midwest and Mid-Atlantic regions, and fulfillment centers that are strategically located near our customer base in major metro areas," Turk said.

Partnering with 3PLs has made this nationwide coverage possible, as well as helped the company minimize transportation, warehousing, overhead, and other costs by maximizing space. Floyd's receives pallets of products that are ready to be fulfilled to the company's 3PL sites, where they are then kitted in cartons, palletized, and stored in rack systems. Not only do the 3PLs need to be able to handle e-commerce volume and speed, Turk said that it was especially important that their partner warehouses also had "the technological innovation to scale with us and provide the best experience to the customer. In terms of efficiency and eventually having this translate into customer satisfaction, Turk has found that from order to fulfillment, "anything we can do to automate the operation is generally a good thing."

Not only is Floyd's product footprint streamlined, so, too, is its overall inventory stockpile: "we're really focused on optimizing every aspect of our operation, so we reduce the amount of inventory we're holding at any point. We hold thirty to forty-five days [worth of merchandise] at a time," said Turk. This allows Floyd pretty significant flexibility, especially for the furniture industry. "We can increase production or decrease production because we're on a more frequent cadence with our manufacturers. A traditional furniture retailer will make big buys of inventory two to four times a year, so if you have an issue, it's really hard to recover."

By designing its company specifically for e-commerce, Floyd has been able to find and create new ways to innovate. New, at least, to the e-commerce sphere is its attention to detail, quality, and customer focus, which marks it as next in a long line of great American design brands. Its awareness and utilization of technology allow it to offer its customers a seemingly old-fashioned thing: a timeless, well-made, sustainably manufactured product, and an exceptional experience.

CASE STUDY: SKIN SCRIPT

Like many successful businesses, Skin Script was designed to fill a gap in the market. Finding professional-grade skincare products difficult to source from big companies with very long shipping times to boot, aesthetician Lisa VanBockern decided to contact chemists herself. With two physicians and four other aestheticians, VanBockern wrote a detailed wish list for skincare products. From that, Skin Script was born and began, pretty quickly, "selling like crazy," said VanBockern. For the first six months, she ran the business out of her house, employing a little grassroots marketing. It wasn't long before she was in competition with the big skincare brands. Now, almost thirteen years later, Skin Script has grown into a company too large for VanBockern to handle on her own, let alone out of her house.

After an initial move into an office "with two assistants," one of whom was the "shipping guy," VanBockern said the company was "still very much homegrown, [with] products everywhere. Inventory was a matter of eyeballing how many boxes you had." When Skin Script finally expanded into a space with warehouse facilities four years after its founding, "even then, we weren't automated—we were just hamsters running in every direction." The final straw forcing her to automate, VanBockern said, was QuickBooks. "It couldn't handle so many transactions; we had to get a bigger system." After a bit of research, the company settled on NetSuite's ERP* (Enterprise Resource Planning) software, and at the advice of Eide Bailly, a NetSuite implementation partner, looked into RF-SMART, "a leader in barcoding and mobile inventory management solutions for warehousing, wholesale distribution, manufacturing, retail and e-commerce," for automating Skin Script's warehouse operations. RF-SMART allowed Skin Script to leverage barcodes and data collection technology to automate warehouse processes, so the production, movement, management, and fulfillment of inventory became fast and accurate.

In its first rollout of newly automated systems, Skin Script had some "hiccups," including manually recoding the data of all its inventory to have matrix barcodes (linear barcodes are those very familiar one-dimensional codes made up of bars of differing widths, while a matrix barcode is usually a two-dimensional square containing a pattern of cells. Matrix barcodes, which can hold far more data than linear ones, are becoming far more prevalent[381]). As employees began using scanners with pick tickets, VanBockern and her team began to notice some efficiency gains, but, she said, "the rest of the processes were still manual."

It wasn't until Skin Script moved into another warehouse space—this time designed and built out specifically to meet the company's needs and RF-SMART's tools that efficiency gains skyrocketed. They implemented bins, as well as RF-SMART's sales order picking which, because it "prompts users to scan product as it's picked...prevents users from picking incorrectly."[382] In addition, Skin Script streamlined its pack stations and shipping processes with pickers scanning at every step of the process and packing and labeling boxes in succession.

Prior to automating, the company averaged 250 boxes shipped per day. Now, says Tim Chapman, Skin Script's shipping warehouse manager, they can do 700 to 800 easily—"one day," he

---

381 Liz Pearcy, "Linear vs. Matrix," *Datalinx*, last modified April 21, 2016, https://www.datalinx.co.uk/blog/linear-vs-matrix.

382 "Skin Script Case Study," *rfsmart*, accessed October 12, 2020, https://www.rfsmart.com/netsuite/case-study/skin-script.

said, "we did over 1,000." A careful consideration and success-ful implementation of automation has enabled VanBockern and Skin Script to effectively quadruple its output. Though the sales and revenue growth that such increases imply are surely appreciated, the customer service gains are what matter most to VanBockern. "Lisa really cares about her customers," said Chapman. "Being friendly, getting [the product] out there," said VanBockern, "we don't even have a marketing team!" With 16,000 accounts and growing, that's some customer service! "Getting products out to customers accurately in a timely manner," is a distinct component of customer service, said Chapman. It's one with which automation, and RF-SMART's WMS solutions, in particular, have helped tremendously.

Enterprise resource planning or ERP software is the system businesses use when they need integration of multiple busi-ness processes, systems, and data. Thanks to advancements in technology and cloud computing, the benefits of ERP systems are no longer reserved for large companies. NetSuite, men-tioned earlier, now offers a small business edition, combining accounting, CRM, and e-commerce businesses into one solu-tion. Furthermore, many ERPs also provide access to a suite of integrated applications serving additional business needs like shipping, tax, warehouse management, business intelligence, and more.

CASE STUDY: TIPSY ELVES

In 2013—some two years after their launch—Tipsy Elves' co-founders Evan Mendelsohn and Nick Morton found themselves in front of *Shark Tank*'s five famous investors, pitching their business as the premier ugly Christmas sweater purveyor. "We didn't know what to expect, but what's there to lose," said Andrew Sutton, Tipsy Elves' head of operations and fulfillment. "It seems like a dream, even to this day," he continued, as Shark Robert Herjavec offered the pair $100,000 for a 10 percent stake in the company, which they accepted. Not only is the company still in partnership with Herjavec—who cites Tipsy Elves as one of his most profitable investments—the episode has become a fan favorite and has been an unusual metric by which the company can track its own growth and evolution: "We had no idea how big the exposure would be, let alone to keep coming back, [with] four to five follow-ups, spin-offs, reruns—the organic growth that has come from that!" said Sutton.

Since filming that episode, Tipsy Elves has expanded considerably, now offering "fun, outlandish products for any and every holiday throughout the year," as well as non-holiday themed apparel, like "ski suits, Hawaiian shirts, golf pants; we outfit people for life's greatest moments with a little more...humor and color," said Sutton. As the Christmas-sweater business is fairly static and seasonal, such expansion has proved fruitful for the company, which is always looking for smart ways to scale and expand. Beyond exuberant apparel, Tipsy Elves is also "gaining a reputation in the promotional product world." It wasn't a move the company had necessarily anticipated, but as more brands came to them for custom gear, and referred others to Tipsy Elves along the way, they've inadvertently begun helping to update the "extremely old-fashioned" and underconsidered industry of what were once logo-emblazoned ballpoints and lanyards.

Its direct-to-consumer business, however, is still central, and Christmas or not, almost all of Tipsy Elves' shipments are time-sensitive in a way that, say, a pair of jeans or shoes are not. Thus, on-time delivery has been an extremely crucial component of the company's success: "80 to 90 percent of our orders are for a specific date, so if they're late, the merchandise is somewhat worthless," said Sutton. When you add to that Tipsy Elves' seasonal fluctuations, outsourcing to 3PLs has been a challenge. Admitting that the company is "not a 3PL's ideal client at all," Sutton has become something of a fulfillment center connoisseur, helping Tipsy Elves move to their fifth and hopefully last 3PL. "Previous partners [were not] able to scale to [our] slowest days of four to 500 orders, [and then] six to 8,000 orders on high days."

With this 3PL, which uses a combination of robotic and human labor, Sutton believes that Tipsy Elves has finally found its ideal partner. The company contracts 50,000 square feet, the majority of which is traversed by Locus Robotics' "segue-type technology, without a human rider." Humans still do the picking and receiving, but robots do the vast majority of the walking, such that "inbound goes up, [and] outbound goes up." The robot "will wheel itself to the needed location, turn a certain color to notify a human associate, [and fly] back and forth to take material back to ship stations." Once the picker has found the needed item, it is placed on the Locus robot's tray, which "wheels back to the ship station."

Of the five 3PLs Tipsy Elves has worked with, Sutton reports that three of them were still using physical pick sheets. Without real-time updates, none of the possible order changes—cancellations, modifications, additional orders from the same warehouse area—are communicable, thus wasting a surprisingly large amount of time in needless or repeated actions. Tipsy Elves' current 3PL uses an "IT-based order routing system connected to electronic devices [that] direct robot or human associates to where they should go."

These and other measures have enabled Tipsy Elves to become far more efficient, as well as hit its desired KPIs, particularly around shipping. From 2018 to 2019, the company experienced 10 percent growth, while maintaining 99.5 percent on-time deliveries, all with "one-third the human beings working the account." Numbers like this have something of a snowball effect, as that impressive on-time delivery rate significantly lowers returns (sub 10 percent), and customer service issues. At the same time, it has boosted Tipsy Elves' NPS, increased their lifetime customers, and led to greater savings overall.

The desire to improve operations while spending less money is the dream of all businesses, and it's one that Tipsy Elves believes is achievable if the timeline for "less money spent" is extended well into the future. Sutton touts the company's investment in ShipHawk software as a good instance of this. By utilizing ShipHawk's carrier optimization, which analyzes a myriad of factors internal to a sale against external carrier rates, Sutton says that Tipsy Elves has "saved north of 20 percent on carrier costs without impacting the customer experience."

Tipsy Elves' belief in the long-term rewards of quality investments and partnerships has led the company away from trying to save money in the short term, which they've found can be a recipe for disaster. Especially when contracting with a 3PL, the decision to invest more up front has paid off hugely for the company: 3PLs' accounts tend to "operate on super small margins," said Sutton, "so they staff low, [and] try to stretch thin." Tipsy Elves' current 3PL, on the other hand, "overstaffs by 8 to 10 percent." While this hiring practice might generate a higher pick/pack fee for its clients, the near 100 percent on-time shipping, reduction in returns and customer service issues, and increased NPS are all a direct result of that premium fee.

Making strategic, long-term decisions requires that companies become fully knowledgeable about not just its own practices, but the practices of the companies it partners with. Rather than "asking for the moon and the stars" of their 3PL, Tipsy Elves understands that the most successful partnership is a win-win situation for both parties: "the better a warehouse does means the more a company can sell." As Tipsy Elves continues to grow, the company's investment in a combination of labor and robotic automation has ensured that they're able to scale smartly and successfully, allowing them to clad people the world over in ugly sweaters, delivered on time for any occasion.

CASE STUDY: SHINESTY

What do you do when your entire business caters to "party clothes" and, overnight, there is a near-universal ban on gatherings over ten, let alone parties? If you're Shinesty, the Denver-based company dedicated to "keeping you outfitted for all of life's social moments," you get on the company group chat.

Started in 2014, Shinesty began as a sourcer of one-off vintage pieces with a keen sense of its own marketing voice. "We found," said Amber Lesser, Shinesty's director of distribution and logistics, "that it was quite difficult and not necessarily worth it to keep up on one individual unit at a time." After coming across a trove of "party suits, and some other fun party gear," the company began dabbling in wholesale while building a considerable clientele base. "Then," continued Lesser, "we started designing our own clothes. We did not start as a private label e-commerce company. That vision developed over time, and now we've evolved a second time into the subscription side of the business." That "subscription side" of Shinesty is primarily for men's boxers, which, in keeping with their unique branding abilities, the company calls "ball hammocks." "We had to shift immediately," Lesser said. "you know, the first week that people started going into quarantine, and sales start declining, you have to [ask], 'Do you want to survive?'"

It was precisely this unique branding ability, which helps crystallize the company's market presence just as much as its actual products, that Shinesty's employees tapped into that company group chat. "We have an iMessage chat with all the employees that [we send] hilarious stuff...One day, someone says, 'Oh my god, are you guys watching this Tiger King thing?' and everyone starts replying, [so] you start watching it and start having hilarious banter through text message." After a couple of days, an idea emerges. In the world of party attire, animal prints are a year-round—not just seasonal—staple, with the company having considerable inventory of cheetah, tiger, snakeskin, and other prints. Staying on top of or ahead of trends—e-commerce or otherwise—is a must for Shinesty. "We're watching the top trends every single day and we see Joe Exotic...we have to get on this!" On shinesty.com's landing page, you can see the eventual outcome of this group brainstorm with a picture of a man and woman, both in big-cat emblazoned swimwear below copy reading, "Unofficial Tiger King Merch." Below the couple: "Totally not rebranded already existing products."

Shinesty's ability to move fast and capitalize on trends—"we've been probably too aggressive at certain phases in our life trying to keep up with potential market trends"—has helped create a team and series of systems that are flexible and creative, all of which has served the company extremely well in this current period. "It really is our team," said Lesser. "We can turn these levers on whenever they're needed. And it generally comes from some absolutely ridiculous conversation that we had internally." The ingenuity behind rebranding existing inventory, while calling attention to that fact, has also re-envisioned those subscription boxers—the company's "bread and butter"—as a work-from-home essential: "WFH=No Pants. Wear better boxers."

Though all Shinesty's ideas may originate internally with its team, the levers the company is able to pull extend far beyond. Recognizing a trend as it's forming enabled the Shinesty team to see the immediate and looming need for masks—an item the company had no previous experience designing, producing, or distributing. "We did not have a vendor," said Lesser. "We found a completely new vendor. We were able to turn on all the switches in our supply chain." This included Shinesty's CEO and CCO tapping their networks for potential mask vendors who could produce a "product in two weeks and who can print with a very wide Pantone." Samples were shipped overnight, and then were circulated—also via express shipping as offices were closed—internally until the team decided on a vendor out of San Diego, all within ten days or less. "Making that happen that quickly—it was the executive team that went out and did that," Lesser said. "As we're ready to make a decision, the designs are being made, inventory [decided] how much do we order, what's safe. Marketing started talking about the designs and how to market them—it all happened right away." They put the masks up on their website as a pre-order concept, where they absolutely exploded.

Shinesty's impressive flexibility is something that Lesser considers an essential aspect of the company, and one that can be found on every level, including the distribution center: "We have the best [DC] team now that we have ever had in the history of this company. Every distribution employee is in it 120 percent every single day when they come in...we're constantly talking about ways to be better—the continuous improvement conversation will never end." This constant quest for improvement doesn't stop with the employees. "In five years, we've had four different [WMSs], and that is because the next one has to be better, it has to be a lot better...if it's not good enough, then we move on." Though distribution is still in-house, outsourcing is also a constant conversation, as are other possible advances in automation including reducing the need for supervisory roles and the number of touchpoints and increasing picking and packing accuracy.

No matter the automation or other source of external improvement, however, Lesser is clear that Shinesty's true innovative strength is in its people. "It's how Shinesty works. It always starts with the people—every single employee is an A-player, every single employee cares." Indeed, the only way for Shinesty to incubate and execute ideas as quickly as they do comes from company-wide buy-in and participation. This sense of cohesion stems, at least in part, from all employees knowing that they have a voice within the company, and that each voice is used to make the whole stronger. "My pickers that have been here for two years," Lesser said, "they come to me with ideas. We have one-on-ones every month—how do we make this better?" It's a question as open to the executive team as it is to fulfillment workers, and one they all continue to ask and answer.

APPENDIX B

ANALYZE YOUR SHIPPING STRATEGY

Former General Electric (GE) chairman and CEO Jack Welch once said, "In real life, strategy is actually very straightforward. You pick a general direction and implement like hell."

So how do you pick a direction?

Much of this book has been about all the options that lay before you, but given the vastness of automating a modern warehouse, it's easy to be overwhelmed by all of the possibilities. To help you make the right decisions, in the right order, we developed this shipping strategy self-assessment. You can take it online at adaptordiebook.com, or you can complete a self-assessment below. Answer each of the following questions as honestly as possible and then calculate your score.

1. Which of the following best describes your current shipping strategy?
   - We use shipping to increase conversion.
   - We use shipping as a way to access new markets.
   - We use shipping as a profit center by marking up shipping costs.
   - We use shipping as a way to increase average order value.
   - We use shipping as a way to delight our customers (under-promise/overdeliver).
   - We use shipping as a blunt instrument for conducting business, nothing more.

2. Which of the following strategies would you like to see your business invest more in?
   - We would like to invest in shipping to increase conversion.
   - We use shipping as a way to access new markets.
   - We use shipping as a profit center by marking up shipping costs.
   - We use shipping as a way to increase average order value.
   - We use shipping as a way to delight our customers (under-promise/overdeliver).
   - Nothing. We are doing all of these things and have nothing we can improve on.
   - Other.

3. Which of the following best describes how your company *feels* about shipping?
   - Shipping is one of our five most important business initiatives as a company.
   - Shipping is an important differentiator for our business.
   - It's valuable to our business, but if it ain't broke, we don't fix it.
   - It's a necessity for doing business and nothing more.

- It's the black sheep of our business. Most of us are afraid to look at it or ask the shipping team questions.

4. Which of the following best describes how you are looking to improve shipping this year?
   - Reduce our negotiated shipping rates.
   - Replace old technology preventing us from scaling.
   - Reduce/eliminate/reallocate resources doing manual processes.
   - We're not looking to improve our shipping operation this year.
   - Other (please specify).

5. Which of the following best describes how your company uses shipping data to inform business strategy?
   - Our entire organization has easily accessible shipping-specific analytics and reports that we use to spot problems and to proactively inform our shipping strategy.
   - We occasionally pull reporting from multiple systems to renegotiate with carriers and hold operations accountable.
   - We've got a general idea of where we stand and how we are performing but nothing formal.
   - We don't have any reporting or visibility beyond our invoices and carrier reports.

6. How often do you benchmark your carrier performance and rates?
   - We are regularly and often optimizing our carriers to ensure the best combination of service and value.
   - We went through an RFP process within the last year.
   - We sometimes look for alternatives and make improvements.
   - Never/once. Not looking to fix something that's not broken.

7. When you receive an order, which of the following best describes how you choose which warehouse to ship from?
    - Our system automatically chooses the right warehouse based on available inventory, items purchased, delivery address, and more to choose the optimal fulfillment location.
    - We choose the warehouse based on the optimal shipping zone.
    - We choose the warehouse based on the delivery address and geographic business rules.
    - We manually assign orders to the warehouse we think is best.
    - We only have one, everything is shipped from that warehouse.

8. After an order is placed, how do you determine the best way to ship it?
    - Our system automatically optimizes for the best rate, selecting parcel or freight as necessary, and implementing our shipping policies.
    - Our system lets us get rates, but the logic is really simplified.
    - We manually shop around for rates.
    - We always use the same shipping method or a general rule of thumb.

9. What shipping related information do you store for your products?
    - We store all information required for shipping, including but not limited to weight, dimensions, HS codes, freight class, NMFC, HAZMAT, and more.
    - We store weight and dimensions for all of our products.
    - We only store weight for each product.

- We don't have any product data stored.
- Everything is manual.

10. What method do you use to determine how to pack shipments?
    - We have hardware dimensioning/custom box making, etc.
    - We use item data to determine the optimal box size.
    - We use basic rules-of-thumb.
    - The warehouse team makes the decision on the fly.

11. How do you create labels and BOLs for your orders?
    - We use built our own shipping solution to create labels and BOLs.
    - We use a built-in ERP plugin.
    - We use a multi-carrier solution to create labels and BOLs.
    - We use carrier or 3PL software (like C.H. Robinson, FedEx Ship Manager, UPS WorldShip) to create labels and BOLs.
    - We manually create our BOLs and get parcel labels by logging into FedEx, UPS, or another carrier's website.
    - Other (please specify).

12. How often do you receive billing adjustments from your carriers?
    - A few times a year.
    - A few times per month.
    - In every billing cycle.
    - All the time. We have to dedicate a resource to manage adjustments.

13. What is your approach to parcel shipping?
    - We optimize across a curated list of global, national, regional, and local parcel carriers to ensure our customers have the best options, and we have the best rates.

- We work with FedEx, UPS, and USPS and optimize based on best rate available.
- We work with both FedEx and UPS to create competition for our business.
- We just use a single carrier (FedEx/UPS) and try to drive down costs in our annual rate negotiations.

14. What is your approach to freight shipping?
    - We use a number of national, regional, and local freight carriers to ensure our customers have the best options, and we have the best rates.
    - We work with multiple carriers and 3PLs and choose the carrier based on cost.
    - We have a few carriers we use for different aspects of business, but the lion's share of volume goes with just one.
    - We just use a single carrier (e.g., FedEx Freight or UPS Freight) and try to drive down costs in our annual rate negotiations.

15. Which of the following best describes your company's approach to shipping technology?
    - We have a budget dedicated to continual improvement of our shipping technology.
    - We conduct an annual assessment of our shipping technology.
    - We review shipping technology every few years.
    - We only review shipping technology when something is broken.

16. Which of the following best describes how you present shipping rates to customers?
    - We use transit-time based rates.
    - We use real-time rates.

- We have a basic rate table (we probably lose money).
- We don't present options; they have to request a quote.

17. What options do your customers see in their buying process?
    - We show customers easy to understand options based on transit and delivery service expectations (expedited, home delivery, appointment setting, etc.).
    - We show customers two to three options they can choose from based on transit time expectations.
    - We show customers exact options from carriers' names they know like FedEx and UPS.
    - We don't give customers shipping options.

18. How do you provide shipment tracking information to your customers?
    - We email a tracking link and provide an on-brand tracking experience.
    - We send customers an on-brand email that contains a link to the carrier's website.
    - We use carriers' systems to send shipment notifications.
    - We do not send tracking information to customers.

CALCULATE

1. No points, but you should have a documented strategy to drive goals.
2. No points, but you should have a documented strategy to drive goals.
3. a. 2 pts, b. 1 pts, c. 1 pts, d. 0 pts. e. 0 pts
4. a. 2 pts, b. 2 pts, c. 2 pts, d. 0 pts. e. 0 pts
5. a. 2 pts, b. 1 pts, c. 1 pts, d. 0 pts
6. a. 2 pts, b. 1 pts, c. 0 pts, d. 0 pts
7. a. 2 pts, b. 0 pts, c. 0 pts, d. 0 pts
8. a. 3 pts, b. 1 pts, c. 0 pts, d. 0 pts
9. a. 2 pts, b. 1 pts, c. 0 pts, d. 0 pts
10. a. 2 pts, b. 1 pts, c. 0 pts, d. 0 pts
11. a. 1 pts, b. 1 pts, c. 1 pts, d. 0 pts. e. 0 pts f. 0 pts
12. a. 2 pts, b. 1 pts, c. 0 pts, d. 0 pts
13. No points, but you should have a documented strategy to drive goals.
14. No points, but you should have a documented strategy to drive goals.
15. a. 2 pts, b. 1 pts, c. 0 pts, d. 0 pts
16. a. 2 pts, b. 1 pts, c. 0 pts, d. 0 pts
17. a. 2 pts, b. 1 pts, c. 0 pts, d. 0 pts
18. a. 2 pts, b. 1 pts, c. 0 pts, d. 0 pts

RESULTS

Before you see your operation's rating, let's break down what the different ratings mean:

A: Your organization has a strong, proactive shipping strategy.

B: Your organization values shipping and is actively seeking ways to improve and scale.

C: Your organization needs to rally around shipping as an initiative before you scale.

Fourteen of the questions are scored out of twenty-eight points:

A = 21 to 28 points
B = 10 to 20 points
C = 0 to 9

A RATING RESPONSE

Congratulations, your business has a shipping operation rating of: **A**. Your business is in the top percentile of profiles we've analyzed. You are making data-driven decisions, are well-positioned for scale, and are proactively reviewing and improving operations. You're doing great, but you can do even better.

Here's what we suggest you do next:

Take your negotiated rates to the next level. Connect with a parcel negotiation expert. Negotiation firms allow you to drive down costs without interfering with business as usual. Negotiations can happen seamlessly in the background and deliver savings as soon as the new rates are applied. You can find a negotiation expert at jeremybodenhamer.com/partners.

Introduce new carriers and services. Consider adding regional parcel providers, USPS consolidators like FedEx Smartpost, UPS Surepost, DHL e-commerce or Newgistics (Pitney Bowes) to further drive down hard costs.

Automate. Automate. Automate. Review your shipping technology and resources to determine what opportunities exist for automation.

Talk to an expert. Even best-in-class operations have areas where they can improve. Our team at ShipHawk recently helped a Nasdaq traded company reduce order processing times by 80 percent. Speak to a member of our team and work with a seasoned expert and discover your untapped opportunities.

Schedule a time at jeremybodenhamer.com/shiphawk.

B RATING RESPONSE

Your business has a shipping operation rating of: **B**. Your business is doing well when it comes to shipping but has room for improvement. Your organization has the right mindset and approach, but it seems to lack the technological framework to reduce shipping costs and achieve the flexibility and scalability you need to compete.

Here's what we suggest you do next:

Review how you are presenting shipping options to customers. Are you letting customers see carrier services and names? This can be detrimental to reducing your shipping costs. We're seeing industry leaders move to transit-time-based shipping options to give customers clear expectations on delivery times while providing the company with the power to upgrade, downgrade, or make appropriate carrier selection.

Are you recovering shipping costs? We all know that shipping isn't free—despite what our customers might think. How are you recovering your costs? Consider charging flat rates, building shipping into item prices, or using more complex business rules to charge the right rates in the right scenarios. At the end of the day, it's all about margin, so you need to make sure you have a clear strategy around how (and when) your costs will be recouped.

Identify your most important shipping KPIs. The old saying, "Measure twice, cut once," is just as important to shipping as any aspect of your business. Are you keeping track of SLA violations with your carrier's service times? Are you reviewing shipping costs as a percent of order value to make sure your contribution margins are healthy? Create a system to regularly review your shipping metrics on a daily, weekly, monthly basis. Not only will it add a new level of accountability, but it will create opportunities you may have never seen before to decrease costs, allocate resources for more important things, and ultimately delight your customers. You can find some suggested operational metrics in Appendix C.

Talk to an expert. Learn about the resources available to help with these efforts. Low lift solutions are within reach. For example, parcel cost-recovery firms will do the carrier service auditing for you. They will take a negotiated percentage of the savings, and you get to keep the rest. No additional work for your team is required.

Visit jeremybodenhamer.com/partners to find the best partners for your business.

C RATING RESPONSE

Your business has a shipping operation rating of: **C**. Your business is either in its infancy, early stages, or shipping is simply a neglected part of your operation. Whatever your reason, now is the time to consider your shipping strategy.

Here's what we suggest you do next:

Commit to improving your shipping operation. Before your organization does anything with shipping, your score indicates that shipping may be a bit of a black sheep for your organization.

Investing and committing to shipping as a strategic advantage for your business is no longer something that just Amazon thinks about. It has become table stakes for e-commerce. Now is the time to get your team aligned from the top down.

Equip your operation with the *right* carrier makeup. Are you dependent on a single carrier? Have you introduced USPS into the mix? Do you have LTL relationships beyond just FedEx and UPS Freight? There are better options out there, and the right carrier mix makes all the difference. This doesn't mean you should add twenty-plus carriers, but make sure you have two to four parcel and two to four LTL carriers in the mix to increase competition among the providers for your business and make sure you have the right service provider for every order.

Evaluate what technology you are using. Are you just using carrier-provided software? While often the cheapest software solution, this makes you dependent on the carrier, which frequently results in higher shipping prices. Or are you using a legacy, seat-based software? What will happen when you hit a peak/spike event like Black Friday? How will you scale up? Finding the right technology starts with asking the right questions. Use this time to evaluate where your systems are strong and where there is opportunity for improvement.

Talk to an expert. Growing pains are real, and your attention is frequently drawn to the hottest burning fire. In today's environment, shipping and fulfillment must make the priority list. The good news is that there are many ways for you to realize quick results.

Visit jeremybodenhamer.com and set up a time to speak with a member of our team who will help you create a Fulfillment Efficiency Scorecard.

APPENDIX C

BASIC OPERATIONAL METRICS

Accurate metrics are imperative to a modern operation. There is no alternative to clear visibility, consistently reported. You may be wondering where to start? I get it. I've been exactly where you are. The list is long, and the insights are not always helpful. Here are some baseline operational metrics to get you started.

Step one is measuring. Step two is to create targets and manage your team(s) to your chosen targets. Don't feel like you have to start with the full list. Select those that are the easiest to access and those that will have the biggest impact and start there. I suggest daily reporting.

BASELINE OPERATIONAL METRICS	SYSTEM OF RECORD
1. Target ship cost (by order, inventory type, and/or carrier) tracked to the penny	TMS, WMS
2. Orders processed per minute/hour	TMS, WMS
3. Orders processed per shift	TMS, WMS
4. Warehouse payroll hours per shift	Payroll system
5. Percentage of shipments shipped with a regional/alternative carrier measured by reduction of ship-+spend (#1 above)	TMS
6. Dimensional weight charges due to improper carton selection	TMS + manual via carrier invoice
7. Variance between quoted and billed amount Measured and reported on an order-by-order basis	TMS + manual via carrier invoice
8. Number of errors processed per shift (damage, mispick, wrong box)	TMS, WMS

BASELINE GROWTH METRICS	SYSTEM OF RECORD
1. Scalability How many pack/ship employees needed to support X growth rate?	Payroll system + TMS
2. Seasonal fluctuation(s) Measured as a percentage of current weekly/monthly shipment volumes	TMS
3. Employee training and onboarding Time spent training employees on warehouse tasks that require decision-making. This is not an advanced training metric. It is meant to measure how long it takes you to get new people up-to-speed in your operation.	(before and after)
4. Spend in IT hours Carrier API maintenance, rules customization, pack-and-ship workflow configurations, etc.	Payroll system + ERP

All metrics that indicate a source system assume 100 percent of metric's volume is managed within that system.

APPENDIX D

QUESTIONS FOR YOUR TEAMS

Not sure how to uncover specific opportunities within your org? Here are some role-specific questions for CEOs or company executives to ask their teams in order to identify opportunities for improvement.

PACK-AND-SHIP QUESTIONS (OPERATIONS)
SMART RATING

- ☐ Have we streamlined multi-online storefront, retail, marketplace, and drop-ship order management?
- ☐ Are we using software to select the optimal carrier and service, or are we using tribal knowledge and/or oversimplified rules?
- ☐ Are we using software to select the optimal distribution point for every order? Remember, some items may be in stock at multiple DCs, while others may only be available at a single location.
  - ☐ Are we considering drop-ship options in this calculation?
- ☐ Are we calculating the shipping cost at the point of sale and

using dynamic software-based rules to configure final shipping costs at checkout?

☐ Are we using algorithm-based rules to ensure the proper carrier and service selection in the warehouse?

☐ Are we labeling shipping options by carrier names (FedEx, UPS, USPS) or by delivery promise (three-day, two-day, one-day)?

SMART PACKING

☐ Do we maintain complete inventory data (weights and dimensions)?

☐ Do we allow warehouse workers to manually select shipping cartons and packaging?

☐ Do we allow warehouse workers to manually select carriers and services?

☐ Do we employ algorithmic-based smart packing?

☐ Are we using pack verification?

SMART DATA AND ANALYTICS

☐ Are we running a multimillion-dollar operation on $200/month shipping software?

☐ Have we used historical data and/or software to determine the ideal container sizes to stock at our packing stations and/or stores (for ship-from-store)?

☐ Are we tracking metrics for returns related to in-transit damage?

WAREHOUSE

☐ What is the average time it takes to process an order, and what is our goal?

- [ ] What is the average per person throughput, and how do we increase it?
- [ ] What opportunities do we have to reduce shipping spend without sacrificing customer expectations?
- [ ] If we ship from a 3PL, do we ship on our own carrier rates or those belonging to the 3PL?
- [ ] Do we monitor and report on pick, pack, and ship rates, as independent metrics, across all distribution channels to ensure cost consistency?
- [ ] Do we monitor and report on delivery times vs. delivery promises across all distribution channels to ensure service consistency?
- [ ] Were our warehouse locations determined by historical buyer location data?
- [ ] Have we done research to determine if we could ship cheaper or faster by adding a second/third/fourth DC (could be company-owned or outsourced)?
- [ ] Do we drop ship?
- [ ] Do we monitor and report on pick, pack, and ship rates across all drop shippers to ensure cost consistency?
- [ ] Do we monitor and report on delivery times vs. delivery promises across all drop shippers to ensure consistency of service?
- [ ] If we operate retail locations, are we set up to ship-from-store?
- [ ] Do we know what our current warehouse capacity is?
  - [ ] At what point will we need more space in our current warehouse(s)?
  - [ ] At what point will an additional DC in a different region make sense?
  - [ ] Do we know if additional square footage or robotics will be a more cost-effective solution?

HARDWARE

☐ Are we using hardware components throughout our fulfill-ment workflow(s)? These include devices like thermal label printers, scanners, scales, dimensioners, conveyors, shipping label applicators, and box making machines.

☐ Are we still using paper picking systems?

☐ Are we still manually measuring and weighing cartons?

☐ Are there any nodes in our fulfillment workflow(s) requiring manual data input?

☐ Have we identified specific nodes in our pick, pack, and ship process that are especially costly (high labor, damage, injury rates)?

☐ What hardware does our Warehouse Management System (WMS) provider support?

☐ What hardware does our Transportation Management System (TMS) provider support?

ROBOTICS

You will need to work with specific hardware and/or robotics vendors in order to obtain robot cost data for comparison. Your immediate focus should be on ensuring you are collecting and reporting accurate data within your current operation. Each area below is a potential point for robotic automation.

☐ Is our picking and material handling equipment outdated and due for replacement?

    ☐ Have we compared replacement costs to the costs of robotic upgrades?

☐ How many SKUs do we inventory in each warehouse?

    ☐ What percentage of those SKUs are conveyable or could be handled with robots?

- Have we measured walk/travel time as a percentage of the labor component of our picking costs?
  - Have we compared forecasted labor rates to the cost of implementing an automated storage and retrieval system (AS/RS)?
- Have we compared hiring and retention costs to the cost of implementing robotics?
- What percentage of our workforce is temporary?
  - Does this percentage increase with seasonal fluctuations?
  - How do our seasonal labor costs compare to the costs of replacing the job functions with robotics?
- How long will it take to realize an ROI on each robotics purchase? How does this compare to alternative automation solutions or sticking with humans?
- What is the current utilization of our available warehouse capacity?
  - Have we analyzed the cost of a robotics investment vs. expanding square footage?

PEOPLE QUESTIONS (EXECUTIVE)
STRATEGY

- Is our business model unique in some way that it would be hard for a large, better funded competitor to copy? Companies like Dollar Shave Club, Glossier, and Parker Clay are excellent examples.
- Are we sharing with our customers and prospects how our manufacturing and/or distribution are unique? Environmentally responsible? Human focused? Parker Clay and TOMS are best-in-class in this area.
- If we are selling on third-party marketplaces that may become direct competitors, are we selling all of our products? Specific/

limited product lines? Remember, the marketplace owns the customers, the communication, and the data.

- ☐ Are we utilizing Amazon's Seller Central (where we maintain more control) or Vendor Central (where Amazon has total control)?
- ☐ Have we established measurable goals for which activities will specifically set our business apart? For example, if the majority of your orders follow email campaigns, you may choose growing your email list as your primary goal.
- ☐ Are we inventing inside the warehouse? If yes, what? If no, why not?
- ☐ Is improving our DC working environment and thereby reducing turnover, hiring expenses, insurance rates, new hire training etc., a committed company initiative?
- ☐ Does our company culture place emphasis on the value of the humans operating the business? Just certain classes/roles? Or are perks being confused with culture and values?

DATA AND ANALYTICS QUESTIONS (IT)
VISIBILITY

- ☐ Are our internal business systems connected? (e-commerce, ERP, TMS, WMS, etc.)
- ☐ Are external data sources connected? (carriers, 3PLs, marketplaces, etc.)
- ☐ Are we using business intelligence/data visualization software?
- ☐ Are we using delivery experience or exception management software?
- ☐ Have we identified key performance indicators (KPIs) that match our organization's objectives to specific targets?
- ☐ Are we monitoring:

- ☐ Buying pattern changes at the SKU level
- ☐ Capacity constraints
- ☐ Carrier costs
- ☐ Labor availability and cost by market
- ☐ Inventory availabilities
- ☐ Ship times
- ☐ Ship times vs. delivery commitments
- ☐ IT spend for operations-specific tasks like keeping systems up, connected, and updated with carrier requirements, rate tables, and services?
- ☐ See additional metrics suggestions in Appendix C.

ACKNOWLEDGMENTS

I was four years old when my dad published his first book. As the son of an author, I spent my entire life with his voice in my head. "All writing is rewriting," and "kill your darlings." It was thanks to my dad that I won my first writing competition in sixth grade for my short story *Ugly Tom*, the story of a school bully with breath "that smelled like the bottom of an unwashed garbage can." I can't find the original story, but I'll never forget that line, just like I'll never forget how instrumental my dad has been in my life and my writing. Thank you, Pop!

I'd also like to thank my beautiful wife, Bethany, the consummate professional. She is the true source of all the good in my life and always willing to tell me when my jokes aren't funny.

And my three boys, who are better than me in every way and who constantly inspire me to be a better version of myself. I hope that one day I can learn to love as well as they love, to laugh as deep as they laugh, and to find joy in all the little things like they do.

I am also grateful for my researcher, Layla Forrest-White. I could not have completed this project without you. You made me look better at every turn.

I also want to thank ShipHawk's VP of product and my close friend, a man who has served in many capacities while we've built the business. Our product, this book, and our opportunities to use our work to make the world a better place would not be what they are without his brilliant mind and thoughtful planning. Thank you, Mike!

And to the Scribe Media team, thank you. To my publishing manager, Kayla Sokol; my editor, Lisa Caskey; and my cover designer, Rachel Brandenburg. I couldn't have done this without your thoughtful and patient guidance.

My final and most sincere thanks goes to the ShipHawk team. Thank you for working with me to build a better tomorrow. Our work has only just begun.

ABOUT THE AUTHOR

JEREMY BODENHAMER is a leading expert at the intersection of shipping and e-commerce. He has been featured in *Inc.*, *TechCrunch, AOL, Fortune, Internet Retailer,* and *Entrepreneur*; is a frequent speaker on innovation, technology, and logistics; and was a 2018 Supply Chain & Executive Pro to Know.

Jeremy is an active volunteer in the community, an avid Crossfitter and surfer, and champion of a company culture that promotes health, family, and happiness among employees. He lives in Santa Barbara with his wife—educator and youth advocate, Bethany Bodenhamer—and their three sons.